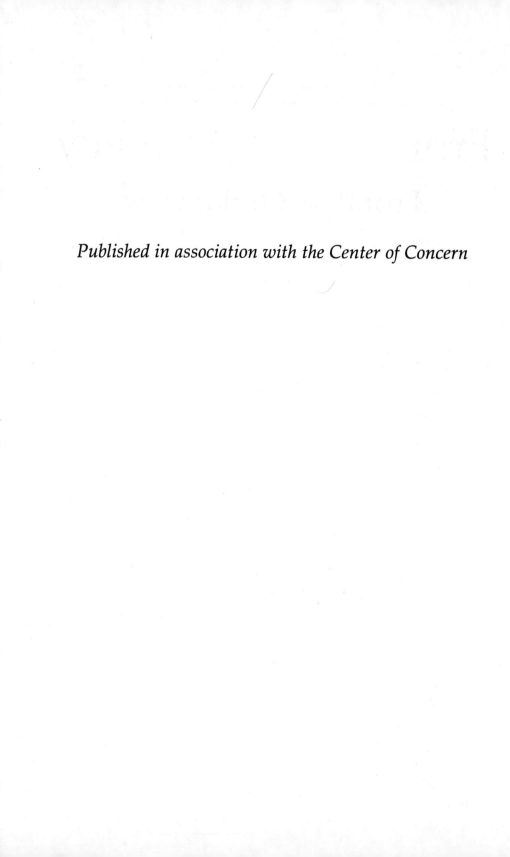

Published in association with the Center of Concern

Frontline Diplomacy
Humanitarian Aid
and Conflict in Africa

John Prendergast

LYNNE
RIENNER
PUBLISHERS

BOULDER
LONDON

Published in the United States of America in 1996 by
Lynne Rienner Publishers, Inc.
1800 30th Street, Boulder, Colorado 80301

and in the United Kingdom by
Lynne Rienner Publishers, Inc.
3 Henrietta Street, Covent Garden, London WC2E 8LU

Library of Congress Cataloging-in-Publication Data
Prendergast, John.
    Frontline diplomacy : humanitarian aid and conflict in Africa /
by John Prendergast.
        p.   cm.
    Includes bibliographical references and index.
    ISBN 1-55587-696-X (pbk. : alk. paper)
  1. International relief—Political aspects—Africa, Northeast.
  2. International relief—Political aspects—Africa, Eastern.
  3. War relief—Political aspects—Africa, Eastern.
  4. War relief—Political aspects—Africa, Northeast.
  5. Africa, Northeast—Dependency on foreign countries.
  6. Africa, Eastern—Dependency on foreign countries.
  7. Conflict management—Africa, Northern.
  8. Conflict management—Africa, Eastern. I. Title.
HV555.A435P74   1996
361.2'6'096—dc20   96-25509
                                                                      CIP

British Cataloguing in Publication Data
A Cataloguing in Publication record for this book
is available from the British Library.

Printed and bound in the United States of America

        The paper used in this publication meets the requirements
    ∞ of the American National Standard for Permanence of
        Paper for Printed Library Materials Z39.48-1984.

5 4 3 2 1

Contents

Preface

Many people deserve my gratitude for the production of this book. First and foremost, appreciation goes to my wife, Jean, who accompanied me into the field half of the time and tolerated my absences or all-night writing sessions the other half. Conceptually, the work of (and working with) Mark Duffield and Mary Anderson influenced my analysis greatly. Collaborating with Colin Scott on a strategy paper for the U.S. Office of Foreign Disaster Assistance also helped shape my views. Gayle Smith, Ken Menkhaus, and Kathi Austin all provided extremely useful critiques of earlier drafts of the manuscript, and Keith Kessler and Renee Storteboom made major research and editorial contributions.

Financial support from the U.S. Institute of Peace made the entire project possible, but the opinions, findings, and conclusions and recommendations expressed in this book are my own and do not necessarily reflect the views of the U.S. Institute of Peace. David Smock of the institute has been instrumental in helping to disseminate the results of my research, and he was a great traveling companion in Sudan and Angola. Similarly, the United Nations Children's Fund (UNICEF) is assisting in the dissemination of the results of this project. Angela Raven-Roberts of the UNICEF Emergencies Unit has been particularly supportive.

This book is a joint production of the Center of Concern and the Strategic Initiative on the Horn of Africa (a project of the Center for Strategic Initiatives of Women). It results primarily from the findings of four field trips to the Greater Horn during 1995.

For reasons of discretion and security, I cannot quote many of the dozens of Sudanese, Somalis, Ethiopians, Eritreans, Djiboutians, Kenyans, Ugandans, Rwandese, Burundians, and Tanzanians who have been key in shaping my views on the subjects covered in the book. I dedicate this work to their quiet commitment in the face of extremely difficult circumstances.

—John Prendergast

Acronyms

AHA	Africans for Humanitarian Action
AICF	Agence Internationale Contre le Faim
CARE	Cooperative for Assistance and Relief Everywhere
CART	Combined Agency Relief Team
CRS	Catholic Relief Services
CSIW	Center for the Strategic Initiatives of Women
DART	Disaster Assistance Response Team (OFDA)
DELTA	Development Education for Leadership Teams in Action (UN)
DHA	Department of Humanitarian Affairs (UN)
ECHO	European Union Humanitarian Office
EPI	expanded program of immunization
EPLF	Eritrean People's Liberation Front
ERA	Eritrean Relief Association
ERD	Emergency Relief Desk
EU	European Union
FAO	Food and Agriculture Organization (UN)
ICRC	International Committee of the Red Cross
IDP	internally displaced
IGAD	Inter-Governmental Authority on Development
JRP	Joint Relief Partnership
MSF	Médecins sans Frontières
NGOs	nongovernmental organizations
NLC	National Liberation Council (SPLM)
NSCC	New Sudanese Council of Churches
OFDA	Office of Foreign Disaster Assistance (U.S.)
OLS	Operation Lifeline Sudan
PRA	participatory rural assessments
RASS	Relief Association of Southern Sudan
RENAMO	Mozambique National Resistance Movement
REST	Relief Society of Tigray
RFPs	requests for proposals
RPF	Rwandan Patriotic Front

SACB	Somalia Aid Coordination Body
SCF	Save the Children Fund
SEOC	Sudan Emergency Operations Consortium
SPLA	Sudan People's Liberation Army
SRRA	Sudan Relief and Rehabilitation Association
SSIA	South Sudan Independence Army
TPLF	Tigrayan People's Liberation Front
UNAMIR	United Nations Assistance Mission in Rwanda
UNDP	United Nations Development Programme
UNESCO	United Nations Educational, Scientific, and Cultural Organization
UNICEF	United Nations Children's Fund
UNITA	National Union for the Total Independence of Angola
UNITAF	United Task Force (Somalia)
UNOSOM	United Nations Operation in Somalia
UNREO	United Nations Rwandan Emergency Office
USAID	U.S. Agency for International Development
WFP	World Food Program
WID	women in development

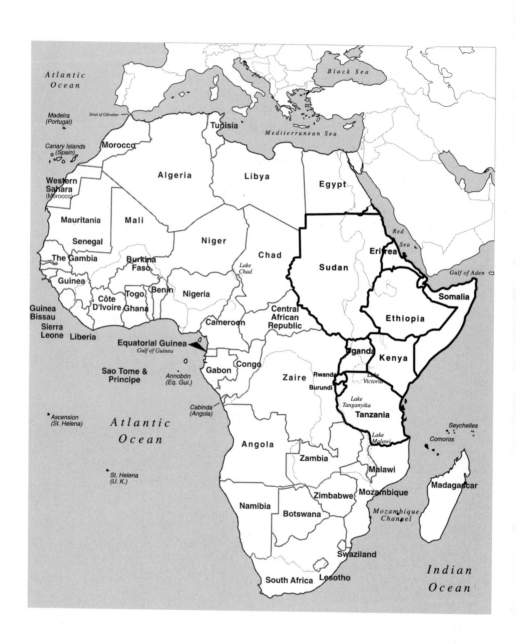

Atlantic Ocean

Madeira (Portugal)

Canary Islands (Spain)

Strait of Gibraltar

Black Sea

Mediterranean Sea

Tunisia

Morocco

Western Sahara (Morocco)

Algeria

Libya

Egypt

Red Sea

Gulf of Aden

Mauritania

Mali

Niger

Chad

Sudan

Eritrea

Senegal

The Gambia

Burkina Faso

Lake Chad

Somalia

Guinea

Benin

Nigeria

Ethiopia

Côte D'Ivoire

Togo

Ghana

Central African Republic

Guinea Bissau

Cameroon

Sierra Leone

Liberia

Equatorial Guinea

Gulf of Guinea

Uganda

Kenya

Sao Tome & Principe

Annobón (Eq. Gui.)

Gabon

Congo

Zaire

Rwanda

Burundi

Lake Victoria

Ascension (St. Helena)

Cabinda (Angola)

Lake Tanganyika

Tanzania

Atlantic Ocean

Seychelles

Comoros

Lake Malawi

St. Helena (U.K.)

Angola

Zambia

Malawi

Madagascar

Mozambique

Zimbabwe

Namibia

Botswana

Mozambique Channel

Swaziland

South Africa

Lesotho

Indian Ocean

1

The Context of Aid in Complex Emergencies: The Seven Deadly Sins

The devastation caused by complex political emergencies (defined as multicausal political crises with major humanitarian repercussions) is creating increasing demands on a global humanitarian response system that will likely have fewer and fewer resources with which to ameliorate suffering or address its causes. And with increasing frequency, questions are being asked about the effectiveness of humanitarian assistance and the extent to which it sustains or prolongs conflict. Whether humanitarian aid actually lengthens conflict beyond its natural course is debatable; but such aid does have indisputable impacts on the course of conflict, and it has become integrated into the dynamics of conflict. It is the aid and policymaking communities' responsibility to learn what those impacts are and how to avoid or even transform them.

This book addresses three issues: how emergency aid can exacerbate conflict; how to minimize aid's fueling of conflict; and how humanitarian assistance might contribute to peace building. Evidence comes from the geographical entity in northeast and east-central Africa that policymakers now call the Greater Horn, which is the focus of a major attempt by the U.S. government at reconceptualizing bilateral and multilateral relations. The new strategy—called the Greater Horn of Africa Initiative—focuses on conflict prevention and food security as its two primary organizing concepts.

The Greater Horn consists of Sudan, Ethiopia, Eritrea, Djibouti, Somalia (and the unrecognized Republic of Somaliland), Uganda, Kenya, Tanzania, Rwanda, and Burundi. The region—rent by periodic famines and even genocide—is in many ways symbolic of the global increase in complex emergencies, and it has pioneered many policy responses to chronic crisis.

Conflict occurs at multiple levels in the Greater Horn of Africa: regional, national, and local. There are currently three major conflicts with regional implications: first, low-intensity cross-border conflicts between Sudan and four of its neighbors (Uganda, Ethiopia, Eritrea, and occasionally Egypt) marked by extensive use of proxy rebel groups; second, the Great Lakes conflagration, a struggle primarily between Hutu and Tutsi elites for the control of Rwanda and Burundi but also involving neighboring governments who side with particular factions as well as border areas rendered increasingly insecure by refugee flows and cross-border military incursions; and third, conflicts among competing Somali factions that affect the Ogaden (Ethiopia's Somali region), Djibouti, northeastern Kenya, the unrecognized Republic of Somaliland (northwest Somalia), and Somalia itself.

National-level conflict has resulted in civil wars in most of the Greater Horn countries during the past decade. Finally, local-level conflict resulting from struggles over local resources has resulted in increasing violence and interrupted livelihoods throughout the region.

The Greater Horn has been a laboratory for innovative crisis response. During the past decade, the cross-border operation into rebel-held territory in Ethiopia and Eritrea, the negotiated access aid agreement in Sudan, and the use of the military in Somalia and Rwanda were all groundbreaking efforts at reaching war-affected civilian populations.

It is important to preface the critique that follows by saying that many of aid's negative impacts result from legitimate dilemmas facing agencies that are operating in extremely difficult circumstances. Many of the challenges highlighted in this book, usually present in natural-disaster situations, are exacerbated and heightened when conflict is present.[1]

The insightful quotations about aid's impacts found throughout the text result largely from interviews with field personnel, not agency headquarters staff. The context for the interviews and for the book itself is one of constructive criticism. The critiques and arguments advanced here are not rationales for stopping humanitarian aid; rather, they are delivered in the hope of improving current analysis and practice.

This kind of evaluation must occur on a regular basis. "Reflection is considered the pastime of academics," notes Kenyan peace activist Kabiru Kinyanjui. "Issues must be discussed transparently to keep these dilemmas in the open."[2] Vincent Coultan, regional advisor for the Cooperative for Assistance and Relief Everywhere (CARE) programs in the Greater Horn, concurs: "Eventually, agencies need to start engaging donors and the public on complex issues, on root causes, on dilemmas. But it's risky when short-term fundraising goals are so overwhelming."[3]

Globally, humanitarian assistance is often caught up in a jungle of competing imperatives that hinder its effectiveness and heighten its potential for producing "negative externalities"—unintended consequences that affect a conflict situation in harmful ways—especially those that to help sustain, or at least intensify, conflict.

This first chapter addresses some of the competing imperatives and structural limitations that litter the context in which humanitarian aid is introduced and that often exacerbate the negative impacts of assistance. As with the remainder of the book, particular reference is repeatedly made to case examples and insights from the countries and people of the Greater Horn.

Sin 1: The Numbers Game

Because of public relations and reporting demands, aid agencies (whether UN agencies, donor-government aid agencies, or nongovernmental organizations [NGOs]) are under constant pressure to portray the huge amounts of aid inputs (food, medicine, etc.) delivered to a targeted population as having a direct impact on saving lives. Consequently, logistical targets become ends in themselves: 1,000 metric tons delivered, 1,000 lives saved, and so on. Reporting and fund-raising priorities partially dictate a quantitative (rather than qualitative) impact assessment that buries nuances and portrays tonnages of commodities delivered as the measure of success. In most emergencies in the health and veterinary sectors, a "grab-and-jab" approach to vaccinations hinders the development of more strategic, integrated planning of interventions.

A multidonor evaluation of the response to the Rwandan crisis concluded that "in a context of increased concern for profile by, and competition between, humanitarian agencies, the objectivity of their reporting may suffer as a result of their emphasis on the positive aspects of their programs and playing down of the negative."[4] David Rieff of the World Policy Institute elaborates: "It takes nothing away from the genuine nobility of the humanitarian impulse to say that even some of the most heroic and seemingly successful humanitarian operations cannot simply be evaluated in terms of their short-term effects, which is the upbeat way in which press reports, not to mention the fundraising brochures of the NGOs themselves, usually characterize them."[5]

Mark Duffield of the University of Birmingham posits two characteristics of a "culture of success" that pervades many aid agencies that face increased competition for funding—often one short-term relief contract after another—and must report successes and eschew doubts. Agencies often tend to (1) restrict evaluations to the project level and downplay wider consequences and (2) measure outcomes by inputs (workshops, medical kits, food aid, etc.).[6] "If you're resource-driven, you identify beneficiaries," says Tanya Boudreau of Save the Children Fund (SCF)—UK. "If you're principle-driven, you identify problems."[7] Far too often, the former mentality prevails.

This "culture of success" measured by numerical targets can make the containment of negative externalities difficult to prioritize. For example, regarding the important objective of targeting, a donor-government field officer summarizes, "If we are feeding the victims of emergencies, the world doesn't care if armies also benefit from relief. Only if the armies are the only ones that benefit does it become a problem."

When responses are logistics-driven, and reaching the highest number of people possible becomes critical for public relations purposes, the effectiveness of containing or preventing complex emergencies is questionable. Problematic responses often stem from legitimate difficulties of evaluation, i.e., diagnosing the relevant causes of crises and what might most effectively address those causes. Logistics-driven programs can limit the scope of response largely to unsustainable inputs that do little to address the communal dissolution and institutional decay that underpin most complex emergencies. Agencies that conceptualize famine relief as logistical operations to address food shortages may, by ignoring famine's role in politico-military dynamics, worsen dysfunctional local power structures that cause or deepen famine.[8]

Sin 2: High-Stakes Fund-raising

The famines that complex emergencies often produce are understandably the biggest-ticket items for agency fund-raising efforts. Emergency responses during the past decades in Ethiopia, Somalia, and postgenocide Rwanda produced remarkable increases in the privately funded portions of agency budgets and led to major surges in public contributions as well, both bi- and multilateral. A 1995 World Peace Foundation conference report concludes, "Rwanda has become a milch cow for NGOs—an enormous fundraising opportunity. Most potent for inducing donations are stories about and photographs of abandoned children and the sick."[9]

Media exposure of an agency's response is often the principal umbilical cord for agency survival and prosperity, so influencing that coverage and the media's access to the famine is critical. (When representatives of the mass media cover complex emergencies, they are often searching for the worst-case pictures—"disaster pornography," as Rakiya Omaar has called it. But often journalists' intentions are not purely exploitative; Ted Turner of CNN is on record as saying that he wants to make suffering people real to the viewing public through television images.[10]) Because of the comparative advantage of famine fund-raising, there is often motivation to publicly present complex emergencies as simple famines caused by drought or (more recently) war. "There is a real famine nostalgia among agencies," charges one agency's former regional director. But these simplistic presentations of famines are shortsighted; they breed cynicism and despair in the public over what appear to be endless crises whose root causes are never addressed. "Sometimes I wonder if we are trapped by our budgets," laments Stein Villumstad of Norwegian Church Aid.[11]

In the context of this nostalgia and despite the learning curve of the past two decades, camps for displaced people are often favored over decentralized initiatives because of their high profile, ease of operation, and photogenic product. "For many agencies, the Rwandan refugee camps were a dream situation," according to the country director of an international agency. As Duffield has highlighted, complex questions of communal adaptation to chronic crisis and the need for institutional support and reform are usually left unbroached. Joelle Tanguy of Médecins sans Frontières (MSF) agrees that this "politics of pity" focuses on suffering, not on the political or social roots of a crisis.[12]

This phenomenon at times reached ludicrous proportions in the response to the Rwandan refugee crisis in Zaire. Kathi Austin, consultant to the Human Rights Watch Arms Project, explains:

> Aid agencies that had never operated in emergencies landed in Goma, bolstered by the media attention to the disaster portrayed on CNN and able therefore to raise membership money. Of the new agencies, few had experience or practical skills. Within two months of the refugee exodus from Giseyni there was an overkill of agencies responding to the emergency scene. This led to an unwieldy implementation program, and the United Nations High Commissioner for Refugees (UNHCR) is still [by the beginning of 1996] having trouble downsizing the number of operations in eastern Zaire.
>
> Many agencies spent incredible sums of money from the beginning on media relations, flying in sympathetic journalists as if on media junkets. These agencies often prohibited access to camps if the sympathy of the journalist could not be assured.[13]

A donor representative decries the current setup: "We are led by the nose by NGOs with their own agendas and desire to raise more funds. Reason is thrown out the window." Though perhaps overstated, this absence of strategic planning by donor agencies for each unique complex emergency is a valid cause for concern. Another donor representative expands on the problems caused by massive media attention to particular crises, noting that the "media coverage—and subsequent public hysteria—promotes this immediate response. Research, analysis and strategic planning are forfeited in the rush to be first. I've seen it happen in Somalia, and despite the many published 'lessons learned' suggesting a more thoughtful initial response, happen again in Rwanda. How can we educate people of the need not to be first?"

The legacy of the 1984–1985 Ethiopian famine continues to cast a shadow over attempts by agency staffs to move beyond sensationalist fund-raising to a sustainable crisis prevention rationale. An NGO head describes the response in Ethiopia to bad rains in 1993–1994:

> The need for publicity causes us to distort the facts. This was out of control in Ethiopia in 1993–94. The shrieking mass of government and NGO representatives chose to call some limited, chronic food shortages a "famine." USAID coddled the government on this and didn't blow the whistle as the famine button was pushed. Headquarters pressured us to respond with a massive emergency program. NGOs should have their licenses pulled for this complicity.

The headquarters of another international NGO operating in Ethiopia repeatedly ran a fund-raising advertisement in 1995 in major newsmagazines such as *Newsweek,* claiming that 5,000 people died in a four-month period in one particular area of the country due to famine and implying that a major emergency had returned. When asked about the depth of the crisis in that area, the NGO's country director said he had not been consulted about the ad, that the organization hadn't helped that area for more than a year and a half, and that there was no humanitarian emergency there. He was flabbergasted that his headquarters had created an impression of the local situation that was clearly taking advantage of public perceptions of drought-stricken Ethiopian children etched into people's minds from the 1984–1985 tragedy. Portraying the worst vestiges of poverty and crisis to raise money is understandably necessary, but, as Ken Menkhaus of Davidson College admonishes, "it is critical to maintain accuracy and credibility" in the process.[14]

Sin 3: The Law of the Tool

An age-old maxim called the Law of the Tool holds true in the disaster response field: The nature of a response is in large part dictated by the tools at hand.[15] Most Western donors maintain agricultural surpluses or commodity support programs serving important domestic constituencies, which make food aid a readily available instrument of response. Similarly, the pharmaceutical industry's abundance of surplus drugs and strong lobby create a logic for drug distribution, particularly when a charitable tax deduction is available. Both the agribusiness and pharmaceutical industries' interests are further served by the long-term goal of creating markets for their products. A confluence of humanitarian, political, and commercial interests are thus served by sending food and drugs as the first line of defense against externally defined famines, no matter what the unique causes of the emergencies might be in each situation.

In southern Sudan in 1994, three Hercules C-130 cargo planes suddenly became available and were borrowed by Operation Lifeline Sudan (OLS, the umbrella consortium for UN and NGO humanitarian operations in war-torn areas of Sudan), despite good harvests in many areas. In some places, the harvests were so good that agencies were hard-pressed to hire porters with food-for-work incentives to unload the aid planes. Ironically, in February of the following year, as the most difficult period of the hungry season commenced, agencies couldn't secure sufficient transport because the Hercules aircraft were tapped for other duties. Moving food was also the priority during the Somali crisis. "The food-getting-through response badly obfuscated the situation regarding what should have actually been done in Somalia," says Willet Weeks, formerly the Horn regional director of SCF—US.[16]

In the initial emergency phase, if an increase in funding is available, many people and assets are hired to expand the response infrastructure. But the availability of funds is ephemeral, making rational adjustments in the response regime extremely difficult. Spending priorities are often determined externally, not by local exigencies. Vincent Coultan of CARE comments,

> Where relief programming is being provided, especially in difficult situations that frustrate swift nationalization of key positions, costs are inevitably high. Agencies naturally take pride in maintaining high-quality, thoughtful, and distinctive interventions, which increasingly include developmentally principled elements in, say, peace or health education, environmental impact mitigation, skills

training, and trauma counseling. However, long-term programs for beneficiaries in high-support-need environments are frequently exposed to the risk of donors suddenly turning off the tap at short notice as new humanitarian crises unfold elsewhere in the world and available monies are spread thinner. While it may be financially prudent, it is also irrationally shortsighted to cut activities to the bare essentials of life-sustaining activities when conflict-resolution exercises and work-skills training, which promote an earlier successful reintegration of refugees, may be the most important and ultimately cost-effective steps in achieving the desired durable solution.[17]

The Law of the Tool is related intimately to the model of relief based on immediate, externally perceived need. The conventional relief paradigm's needs-only approach (measuring the severity of a crisis by what inputs might be needed: food, medicine, etc.) masks the structural causes of protracted internal civil conflict and helps deepen and perpetuate the crisis. The model fails for several reasons: It ignores outsiders' historical roles in shaping the unequal internal relations that characterize the crisis; it restricts ownership of program activities to external agencies rather than focusing on the need for local communities to rebuild their own society; and it fails to provide the relational analysis necessary to identify strategic intervention opportunities.[18]

Sin 4: Humanitarian Aid as a Cover

Critics ever more frequently charge that donor governments are using humanitarian aid as a cover for a lack of political engagement. Jean-Christophe Rufin calls this the "humanitarian trap."[19] Foreign policy responses to complex emergencies have underplayed the complexity of the forces driving modern conflicts. They have focused on material aid to ameliorate present suffering and often have not addressed the difficult policy options that might assist in preventing future conflict. Kathi Austin describes this phenomenon with regard to the Rwandan genocide and its aftermath: "Goma's appeal to donors and aid agencies was as much as a palliative for failed intervention during the genocide as it was to prevent a medical epidemic. Sending in the U.S. military and giving the humanitarian effort a 'new' military look was planned to gloss over the U.S. policy failure to prevent and stop the genocide."[20]

"The fault does not lie with the food but with those throwing food at political problems," asserts a donor field officer. In many complex emergencies, donors avoid tough political issues and delivering humanitarian aid to massage symptoms and assuage consciences. "Our humanitarian agenda fills a political void," claims Ted Chaiban of Catholic Relief Services (CRS).[21] Furthermore, as Vincent Coultan points out, "The more effective international agencies in Rwanda are engaged in their traditional forte of strengthening the basic livelihoods of those most vulnerable, but we're not investing in political solutions."[22] Part of the reason for this phenomenon parallels the post–Cold War decline in strategic importance of many regions now engulfed in conflict, many of which were major Cold War flash points and recipients of billions of dollars of military aid.

The critique often goes further and blames humanitarian agencies for not dealing with political roots of crises, a criticism that overestimates agency mandates and their potential for addressing macropolitical issues. "People dump their political garbage on NGOs," observes Geoffry Loane of the International Committee of the Red Cross (ICRC). "There is an illusion that our aid is driving the agenda. But aid is in reality just a by-product of a specific politico-military context."[23] This context is situated in a broader phenomenon of ignorance and lack of respect for the differing mandates of different kinds of agencies created for different purposes. There is a lack of international coordination in creating a rational division of labor and cohesive policy among organizations with mandates that include humanitarian action, human rights advocacy, peace building, peacemaking, peacekeeping, and peace enforcement. Within these different categories, the actors range from those who operate from principles of strict neutrality to those motivated by liberal solidarity.

For example, much of the physical infrastructure is in place for caring for Rwandan refugees and even repatriating these refugees from Zaire and Tanzania. But donors are providing relatively limited resources to address the deeper political issues that prevent the refugees' orderly return, such as the restructuring of the economy, property ownership, the legal framework of mass detentions, and the issues of borders and power sharing. Until more resources are directed to those issues by donors and, to the extent possible, by aid agencies, it is unlikely that any humanitarian strategy will lead to significant repatriation.

Sin 5: The Primacy of Humanitarian Access

In the context of this substitution of humanitarianism for political engagement, the imperative to gain humanitarian access (access for aid agencies to at-risk populations) often takes precedence over advocacy for justice, human rights, and international humanitarian law. This situation leads to the perverse reality that the more burning and killing is done against local populations, the more resources will be sent in to respond. Furthermore, an NGO country director comments, "You can push us around, you can murder our staff, you can steal the food, and we will still come back." Another agency official suggests,

> If donors were to issue a joint statement to warring factions that adherence to humanitarian and human rights principles would be a factor taken into account when making decisions on aid, the impact would be great. Instead, what happens is the opposite: The NGOs feel a great pressure to keep their heads down, even in the face of gross violations, and get on with their projects so as to keep their donors happy and increase the chances for more funding.

Giving priority to humanitarian access in complex emergencies restricts maneuvering room for peace activism in three major ways. First, it reduces warring parties' responsibility for their constituents' welfare. Second, it can indirectly fund conflict through diversion of aid. Third, it often legitimizes warring parties and gives them a formal basis for deflecting criticism.[24]

In the process of negotiating humanitarian access, balance and political expediency usually take precedence over objective, independent assessment. Often aid ratios are determined on the basis of maintaining evenhandedness among warring parties rather than on empirical evidence of need. At times further complications result when aid organizations capitulate to the inevitable invocation of sovereignty and the demands for favorable treatment by host governments in situations of divided governance. In such cases, both independent assessment *and* balance take a back seat to political expediency, i.e., satisfying host-government demands.

In Sudan, the humanitarian agenda of keeping access open at all costs conflicts with calls for a stronger response to counter the massive human rights violations by the Khartoum regime as well as to the fratricidal internecine conflict among southern rebel commanders, which reached its apex in 1991–1993. Most external pressure put on Sudan during the past few years has been on behalf of humanitarian access, not peace. The UN named a Special Envoy for Humanitarian Affairs despite the presence of strong humanitarian diplomats in Philip O'Brien, Cole Dodge, and the late Jim Grant but as of early 1996 had yet to assign someone to address the political roots of the crisis. This lack of political engagement exists despite a request from the (renamed) Inter-Governmental Authority on

Development (IGAD) for a UN official with a political brief. IGAD is the regional organization in the Horn that addresses issues of common concern to Sudan, Somalia, Ethiopia, Eritrea, Djibouti, Kenya, and Uganda, although in March 1996 the organization extended an invitation to other countries in the Greater Horn to join its newly reorganized structure.

Furthermore, the humanitarian-access-first approach has failed entire segments of the population, such as the people of the Nuba Mountains, who have been subjected to scorched-earth forced displacement and extrajudicial executions that should be classified as acts of genocide. Maintaining the guise of neutrality in the face of stark aggression often encourages the aggressor to further pursue military solutions.

One UN food monitor in Sudan headed assessments that led to the dumping of food into two southern Sudanese government-controlled garrisons, supplies that not only mostly benefited soldiers but also were delivered at strategic moments in the conflict. In the first case, food was delivered into a town just before it was besieged by the Sudan People's Liberation Army (SPLA), helping the Sudanese government to withstand the assault on that town. In another case, OLS delivered 460 tons of food to a town just before renegade rebel commander Kerobino Kuanyin Bol launched an asset-stripping and village-burning spree from that town. A *tukul* (hut) count—not a head count—was done to justify this delivery despite an earlier, more careful assessment that had determined there was no humanitarian need. This case illustrates the problem that the strict standards of accountability, transparency, and assessment that have been strenuously advocated in the southern sector of OLS (serving mostly rebel areas) have not been assiduously pursued in the northern sector (for the most part serving government areas), which in this case carried out the flawed *tukul* count.

More broadly, despite substantial grain surpluses and exports recorded in and from the government-controlled area of Sudan, pockets of shortfall in the north during the past half decade received large amounts of aid because of efforts to balance the aid response between northern and southern Sudan.

Despite the sporadic efforts of aid agencies in monitoring their distribution processes at the local level, aid is often distributed formulaically based on social hierarchies. Duffield elaborates:

> Attempts at targeting by aid agencies working through local actors has commonly fallen foul of [formulaic distributions]. The frequent lack of end-use monitoring in emergencies, however, tends to obscure this situation.

The operation of the internal socio-political dynamic of a protracted crisis is largely hidden from aid agencies. When its functioning is glimpsed, however, its exposure is often omitted in NGO and UN reports. Fear of alarming donors, or wishing to avoid casting doubt on the ethos of success that usually surrounds agency projects, are common reasons. The outcome is that practitioner reporting in Complex Political Emergencies is often poor and uninformative.[25]

Knowing that the need for humanitarian access comes first, warring parties often use negotiated access agreements to build credibility in international circles and deflect criticism about their tactics of war. Representatives of influential news media are often present for humanitarian cease-fire signings. "Credibility with the international community is [such parties'] major benefit" from humanitarian access agreements, observes Philip O'Brien, former coordinator of OLS.[26]

Sin 6: Exploiting Competition

Humanitarian organizations responding globally to complex emergencies have proliferated over the past decade in a completely unregulated manner. "Disaster response is a boom industry," proclaims Rowland Roome, country director of CARE—Rwanda.[27] This proliferation creates remarkable inefficiencies, overheads, and sometimes corruption. Mark Bradbury explains,

> The proliferation of NGOs involved in disaster relief has increased inter-agency competition for market resources. This has created a tension between the need for greater coordination and the need to maintain an independent profile. Competition erodes the possibilities for collective action, while the conditionalities of sub-contracting relations subverts the quality of public debate and the ability of NGOs to act as critic and witness.[28]

Moreover, warring factions are often able to easily exploit the competition that logically results from dozens of agencies trying to obtain front-row seats in the response to complex emergencies. Less experienced agencies are often manipulated into operating in areas or ways that maximize benefits to warring parties. High staff turnover and lack of institutional memory among many agencies simply heightens their vulnerability to exploitation and increases the mistakes made because of the absence of a proper analysis of conflict.

There is no institutionalized mechanism to learn the lessons each intervention provides.

"In the case of the Rwandan refugees in Zaire," points out Kathi Austin, "competition was generated between some French-speaking aid agencies and English-speaking agencies. This left the French-speaking agencies more vulnerable, and this vulnerability was capitalized on by the former Rwandan regime and its military in getting some of the Francophile agencies to help supply them."[29]

After visiting an area of southern Sudan where he encountered some NGO workers who questioned why they were working in that area, David Rieff interviewed a particularly forthcoming regional director of the NGO Agence Internationale Contre le Faim (AICF). After Rieff mentioned the frustrations of the field workers, the regional director replied, "The problem is that while there is little for them to do up there, the guerrillas want us to keep a presence in the area, and for our own reasons we need to do so. . . . My job is to assure AICF's survival. If we are out of Sudan [and other agencies replace us], then the hard truth is we are less likely to get funding. . . . That's the reality. An NGO simply must be in certain areas that the donors are paying attention to."[30] Although all agencies would not agree that they are driven to this degree by competition for funding, these comments do indicate the pressures facing agencies that can be exploited by astute warring parties.

"Agencies are just doing their own programs," says one local representative of an NGO operating in Somalia. "They often don't care about local complexities. They make mistakes, creating conflicts with local parties that escalate until the agency is forced to withdraw. If you're going to work in a conflict situation, you have to take all local perspectives into context."

Sin 7: Lack of Accountability and Professionalism

This proliferation of agencies creates huge discrepancies in the agencies' adherence to basic humanitarian principles. Accountability is one such victim. Agencies (or donors) that do not demand full accountability for themselves and their local partners help reinforce relief-dependent responses to crises. These relief-dependent cultures can reinforce military elites and undermine subsistence cultures that favor traditional or civil authorities. Invariably, the less of a stake communal structures have in a given response, the less accountable that response will be.

Conversely, warleaders usually have a stake in the continuation of conflict. For example, the government in Sudan "needs a *jihad*. They're selling tickets to heaven to rich Muslims," says a donor representative. Benefiting from the asset-stripping and -consolidation afforded by continuing instability, warleaders are often most easily sustained in the field by diverted relief inputs, which decreases those leaders' accountability to local populations.

In the context of state turmoil and breakdown in Rwanda and Somalia, NGOs had a hotline to the media and were able to offer political and social analyses that often went unchallenged. Twelve agencies had budgets of more than $10 million in Rwanda during fiscal year 1995. CARE had $14 million to spend over twelve months, more than the government's budget. This amount of money places unparalleled responsibilities on the shoulders of agencies that may be unprepared for the multiple missions created by such a resource imbalance. It also raises serious questions regarding whom these agencies are accountable to. To what extent are agencies accountable to beneficiaries of their programming, and what mechanisms for canvassing beneficiary viewpoints are integrated into agency programming? In the rush to respond to emergencies, these critical questions are usually not fully addressed.

The lack of accountability and professionalism is actually logical in light of reporting and fund-raising prerogatives. Duffield explains:

> In terms of improving an agency's market share, relaxed reporting standards can have an undoubted utility. An indirect community of interest can emerge between protracted crisis and agency advancement. Given that there is no accountability between aid agencies and so-called beneficiaries, and that aid workers adhere to no recognized professional standards, one can argue that not only has the aid market expanded, it is a markedly deregulated one. . . .
> Because of poor reporting and lack of accountability, there is no direct correlation between rising relief expenditure and increasing need. . . . An unknown proportion of rising relief expenditure . . . is market driven.[31]

The professionalism of an emergency response is highly uneven, varying from agency to agency and even within agencies. The multidonor Rwanda evaluation concluded that some agencies "sent inadequately-trained and -equipped personnel, some undertook to cover a particular sector or need and failed, and others were unwilling to be coordinated. The conclusion drawn by the study is that the current mechanisms for ensuring that [agencies] adhere to certain professional standards are inadequate."[32] At the most basic level, the study found, "Experience from complex emergencies has shown that

behavior of staff and the way they choose to interact with the beneficiary community has a major influence on the refugees' and their
own security."[33]

Until the twin issues of accountability and professionalism are
fully addressed by aid agencies, attempts to minimize the negative
effects of aid will be undermined.

2

Good Intentions on the Road to Hell

Sun Tzu's *Art of War* noted the use of food as a military tool nearly three thousand years ago.[1] Aid analysts and providers are increasingly recognizing the extent to which internationally donated food not only is used as a weapon of war but also at times inadvertently helps sustain conflict. Mary Anderson's thought-provoking "Ten Points" in her essay "International Assistance and Conflict: An Exploration of Negative Impacts" galvanized the attention of many agencies, spurring numerous in-house and interagency consultations as well as a number of conferences and workshops delving into the issue in greater detail.

David Keen admonishes agencies and donors that they should seek out the political functions of famine—rather than assume its economic origins—and cautions that those who fail to address the underlying local processes and power structures that create famine and control its relief may only reinforce those power structures and intensify suffering. Such reinforcement may be direct, as combatants exploit relief for military use, or indirect, as they manipulate population movements or render credible their denials of disregard for the populations they control.[2]

Aid sustains conflict in three major ways: Aid can be used directly as an instrument of war; aid can be indirectly integrated into the dynamics of conflict; and aid can exacerbate the root causes of war and insecurity. This chapter will elaborate on these three themes.

It should be noted that these are *potential* negative externalities that have been demonstrated in certain locations after my independent assessment. In no way should this concept be interpreted as positing that all humanitarian aid has all of these effects. Problems are very location specific, as are solutions. The universe of potential obstacles is presented here as a guide for practitioners and policymakers about what to be wary of or to avoid. Many agencies are fully aware of these potentialities and are addressing them creatively, as will be shown in the following sections.

17

Aid as an Instrument of War

Manipulation of Access

In many conflict situations, warring parties deny or block access by humanitarian aid agencies, control access to serve political or military strategies, or directly attack relief infrastructure and personnel.

Throughout the Greater Horn, governments have often invoked their sovereignty to attempt to control or deny access to certain parts of their countries, especially the areas controlled by rebel forces. Rebels have reciprocated by using violence to limit aid flows into government areas. Throughout the 1980s, the Ethiopian and Sudanese governments limited aid to rebel-held areas, a primary reason for the killing famines in 1984–1985 and 1987–1988, respectively. In Burundi today, competing militias have restricted access to civilians in competing areas. MSF estimates that violent restrictions on agency access in Burundi have increased the ratio of dead to wounded to 10:1, as opposed to the average of 1:4 dead to wounded in other wars in which the group is operating.[3] Stein Villumstad explains, "There are different reasons for a government to deny international staff access, but from a humanitarian point of view the most serious is 'witnesses to atrocities are not wanted.'"[4]

Warring parties are becoming increasingly sophisticated and more sensitive to charges of using food as a weapon. Now, instead of overtly blocking aid to areas of contested control, they frequently attempt to directly control (and benefit from) the access routes to those areas. For example, the government in Sudan is attempting to close down the southern sector of OLS and route all aid through government-held towns, even aid destined for rebel-held territory. At the very least, the government will likely succeed in further consolidating its control and veto power over aid movements.

Beyond simply blocking access, many warring parties attack food aid, production, and marketing. Joanna Macrae and Anthony Zwi ascribe three functions to attacks on food in counterinsurgency wars: political, as undermining production leaves populations dependent and compliant; economic, as all famines benefit some merchants or other powerful groups; and military, as warring parties come to see the civilians on whose support rebels depend as targets.[5] In five African complex emergencies, Macrae and Zwi found disturbing tactical similarities among warring parties who made attacks to "quicken the pace of destitution by blocking coping strategies."[6]

The number of attacks on the humanitarian infrastructure—assets and personnel—is increasing rapidly, especially in the form of hostage-taking. Objectives for these attacks include: dissuading agencies from operating in a particular area or serving a particular population (as with the placing of landmines and killing of relief workers in Goma, Zaire); forcing agencies and/or the international community to recognize the presence or legitimacy of the attacking faction (southern Sudanese rebel faction leader Lam Akol unsuccessfully tried to use the denial of safe passage for food-aid barges on the Nile River to receive some form of recognition); cutting off outside aid to populations who are providing sustenance to opposing authorities (the former Ethiopian regime during its war against Eritrean and Tigrayan liberation movements); and the ratcheting up of violence to increase the need for agencies to buy into the extortionist protection rackets connected to military authorities (business as usual in Somalia).

Sometimes a mix of all of these objectives exists. Burundi has perhaps become the most dangerous country in the Greater Horn for aid operations. At least ten aid workers were killed in 1995, and dozens of grenade attacks, ambushes along roads, landmine incidents, and armed assaults have occurred. Many agencies have restricted their operations to Bujumbura, and some have withdrawn most of their expatriate staff. More violence is fueled by an active rumor mill that spreads suspicion against aid agencies. The head of one agency's program expressed frustration about the conundrum in which aid providers find themselves: "If we speak out about what's happening to us and to the people of Burundi, we're likely to get into more trouble, to be subject to more attacks. On the other hand, we can't cower like sitting ducks, waiting to be killed."[7]

Here again, some authorities are smart enough not to do the dirty work themselves but rather to hire mercenary militias to do it for them. For example, the renegade rebel commander Kerobino Kuanyin Bol is paid by the government of Sudan to wreak havoc and divert aid in parts of Bahr al-Ghazal, seriously disrupting OLS activities.

There has also been widespread militia fraud and intimidation, which has distorted refugee registration in Rwandan refugee camps—particularly in Kibumba but also in others—culminating in threats to expatriate staff and the pullout of MSF—Belgium in February 1995. Similar events have also occurred in the camps in Ngara, Tanzania, where UNHCR had to nullify a major registration of beneficiaries.[8]

Manipulation of Population Movements

Warring parties regularly use civilians as shields or food sources for garrisons or training centers. Food is a critical input in mounting operations and defending garrisons, and the more easily accessible it is, the better for a military unit. Macrae and Zwi note that although it is difficult to document (and to overcome donors' reluctance to publicize) abuses in food provision, governments and military forces do selectively provide food to present and potential supporters or populations they seek to lure—or drive—to areas they control.[9] A rebel official told an aid worker, "We can lose the NGOs, but we can't lose the World Food Program [WFP],"[10] indicating the primary position food holds in the hierarchy of attractive inputs.

Factions also position civilians or airstrips to enhance the ability of troops or militia to remain in areas that otherwise might have to be abandoned for lack of supplies or difficulty of defense. In many places, "They're there by the grace of the relief inputs," remarks one donor official. Whether in a border area where military resupply occurs or an interior location that couldn't be resupplied by a military group's own logistical capacity, the location of civilian populations is constantly subjected to cost-benefit calculations by authorities. Again in this case, the civilian feeding centers or distribution points and the agencies serving them act as a protective cover; when they are attacked, the attack is not just against a military garrison but also against the entire aid system.[11]

There are many rationales for these tactics. Besides the protection afforded by humanitarian operations, reserves of manpower are conveniently drawn upon for fresh recruits for military missions. Leaders are often able to establish themselves as "legitimate" authorities in the eyes of civilian populations by drawing aid providers to a particular location, in a "hearts and minds" campaign conducted by that authority. The benefits are so great that in some cases warleaders deliberately exacerbate malnutrition to attract more aid. For example, orphaned children in Lafon in southern Sudan were not fed for weeks by the local South Sudan Independence Army (SSIA) commander in a crass effort to extract additional aid from agencies in the area. The boys were rescued after a few had already died.

In the case of the Rwandan camps in Zaire, the defeated government in Rwanda organized the massive refugee flight into neighboring countries, using civilian populations as their shield. Aid now helps maintain the former government's control over populations that otherwise might have dispersed or tried to go home. Leaders of the military bases at Lac Vert and Panzi kept children on the premises to ensure access to aid; an orphanage was even set up at one camp to keep the aid flowing. The military camp of Bilongue was established just a few kilometers from the civilian camp Chimanga in order to ease access to aid. Many of the cross-border military incursions into Rwanda emanate from these camps. Furthermore, camps remain near national borders despite agency regulations and international protocols opposing this practice.[12]

Some analysts say there is little choice but to provide aid when humanitarian need is great, as was the case when Rwandan refugees poured into Zaire and Tanzania in mid-1994. After that initial phase, some advocate withdrawal from untenable circumstances after an emergency is ended: "We became the quartermaster for the Hutu militia," says Andrew Natsios.[13]

Moving a large displaced population along the Sudan-Uganda and Sudan-Kenya borders has enabled the SPLA to be constantly assured of a food supply line in strategic locations from aid agencies serving the displaced. No simultaneous head counts are ever done of all locations where displaced or refugee populations reside, so there is no certainty about the actual number of beneficiaries. Major trading circles develop around these locations, involving cross-border trade and multiple uses of an infrastructure for military, humanitarian, and commercial purposes. "We deliver enough food aid to feed most soldiers in Equatoria," observes an agency official. John Garang himself allowed that the strategic town of Nimule might fall to government forces if the displaced population on the Uganda-Sudan border were to move too far away from the Nimule area.[14] A similar analysis can be made of the Rwandan relief camps in Zaire, close to the Zaire-Rwanda border.

In another example, the leader of the splinter rebel faction SSIA, Riek Machar, used international relief agencies to help create a forward garrison in Yuai to act as a buffer zone for his principal garrison in Waat. In October 1992, Machar urged the UN to send food into Yuai, which he said was ideal for fishing and had a dry-season river. By January 1993, people were organized by Machar's forces to move south from Waat to Yuai before any relief had been provided. When thousands of civilians in need of assistance began arriving in Yuai, some NGOs and the WFP felt they had no choice but to begin airlifting food and medicine to the area, which created even more of a draw for civilians. At the time, Machar controlled all three points on the Triangle (Kongor, Ayod, and Waat) as well as Akobo to the east. He moved his headquarters to Yuai, which appeared to be well insulated by his garrisons as well as thousands of civilians being served by international agencies. One relief official with a long military background described the arrangement as "brilliant military strategy." When SPLA forces attacked Yuai in April 1993, killing hundreds of civilians, press accounts described the attack as one on a relief center rather than a military garrison, precisely as Machar intended.

In Rwanda, the Rwandan Popular Front grouped together civilian populations in camps for protection in April and May 1994. A number of agencies responded on humanitarian grounds, but an agency representative points out that the operation "was a disaster in terms of engagement." In another part of the country, Operation Turquoise allowed for the harboring of major killers within camps for displaced civilians protected by French soldiers. "The operation helped the militia get out with their arms," avers a donor official.

Mozambique exemplifies the profundity of international relief's effects on civil wars: the Mozambique National Resistance Movement (RENAMO) benefited from the lack of large-scale aid to government areas in 1986–1987 only to see expanding aid subsequently facilitate governmental military control of the north by enabling large populations to live in government areas and leave RENAMO areas and by bolstering the government's legitimacy, the army's logistical support, and the local economy.[15]

Diversion

Warring parties frequently divert humanitarian inputs—especially food and drugs, given their ease of monetization (sale for money)—for their own consumption, for barter or sale, and even for export. Selling or trading diverted commodities across borders is a principal method of obtaining arms. Unlike the manipulation tactics described in the previous section, diversion negatively impacts any "hearts and minds" strategy because it makes the authority less accountable to and reliant on local populations.

An African Rights report explains the advantages to warring parties of diverting aid:

> Civilians have weaker property rights over aid supplies than over their own produce; so appropriation of relief by the army creates fewer tensions.
>
> Aid supplies can often be collected in bulk—e.g., by the truckload—from a relief camp or central store. This is quicker, less traumatic and administratively simpler than taxation or requisitioning from the population at large. Moreover, it centralizes the control of food at the level of the commander, which helps the maintenance of military discipline.
>
> Aid includes commodities (such as medicines) whose procurement and transportation from other sources is difficult to arrange.
>
> Using aid supplies reduces the security risk to the armies of transporting commodities . . . , as regards both interception and the tracing of suppliers.[16]

In Sudan, the three main warring parties all have perfected diversion as a principal strategy of resource accumulation. Looting of rail, road, and barge convoys is rampant. In one theft in 1994, 1,750 metric tons were stolen from a barge. Warehouses and compounds are frequently looted. Distributions are usually targeted, and diversion also occurs through taxation, inflated assessments of number of recipients, and outright stealing.

By early 1993, it was evident that a pattern had emerged in which major diversion of food aid by the SPLA was a particularly acute problem in the area in which that army's main garrison was headquartered. For example, it was commonly alleged that one out of every three Catholic Relief Services–supplied sacks of grain going to areas of the East Bank, including the Triple A (Ame, Atepi, and Aswa) displaced camps, was being diverted by the SPLA, and nearly all of the cooking oil was being diverted and sold in Uganda[17] or traded for petroleum products.[18] In late 1992, one head count found about 83,000 displaced civilians in the Triple A camps, despite the SPLA's claim of 256,900. UN convoys to the area were suspended in October 1992 after the murders of three relief workers and a journalist in which SPLA commanders were implicated, but Norwegian People's Aid and Catholic Relief Services expanded their deliveries to pick up the slack. The cycle of impunity continues.

This situation was similar to the problems faced during the late 1980s and early 1990s in Gambela refugee camps in Ethiopia, and then from 1991 to 1992, when Torit served as the main garrison for the SPLA—Mainstream and food aid was being taken by the SPLA and traded for tires and fuel. World Vision finally had to suspend its activities in eastern Equatoria in November 1992 because of "accountability" problems. When Torit was the garrison, World Vision and Catholic Relief Services were constantly attempting to improve monitoring and accountability and at times had to temporarily suspend operations, such as in November 1991.[19] Diversion was so blatant and widescale that one official speculated off the record that Garang himself must have been told by U.S. officials that their indirect support of him (at that time) would come in the form of plentiful food assistance, which is easily diverted and bartered.

The SSIA also significantly diverts relief supplies. There is regular "taxation" of civilians in the form of a percentage of their relief distribution, an observation not denied in my discussions with SSIA commanders. In SSIA-controlled Nasir in 1993, food was diverted by SSIA soldiers going house to house and taking food, medicine, and fishing materials, despite the presence of twenty food monitors. More blatant looting has also occurred. A donor-government official obtained information that before an SSIA attack on Kongor in late July 1993, the SSIA commander had delayed the attack in order to wait for 600 bags of diverted UN grain to be carried to their forward position.

In Somalia during 1991–1992, major diversion was part of every agency's cost of getting access. But there the diversion was so extreme it was often an end in itself and directly fueled much of the violence in 1992. Natsios writes,

> Food had become the medium of exchange and a principal source of wealth in Somalia. Because food was so scarce both from drought and civil conflict, its absolute value had risen to an extraordinarily high level. This factor combined with the collapse of the economy causing mass unemployment and a dramatic drop in family income increased the relative value of food. This meant food imported through the relief effort became an enormously attractive objective of plunder by merchants, by common working people without a source of income, by organized gangs of young men and by militia leaders in need of the wealth represented by food aid which they would use to purchase more weapons and keep the loyalty of their followers.[20]

In Somalia, Alex de Waal points out other methods of diversion: registering nonexistent villages, forming false committees to represent—and sell food meant for—real villages, and coercing signatures for food deliveries that were in fact diverted. Militias and bandits "looted, pilfered, diverted, or extorted" far more than official estimates of the amount of aid lost—over half, some village-level indigenous relief workers claim.[21] Former Rwandan government and military officials in the Zairian camps used the "cellule" structure to divert food.

Delayed or flawed registration also aids diversion. Zairian Caritas' experience in the Kituku camp shows the importance of credible refugee registration. Rejecting UNHCR population counts, the agency divided WFP food for an estimated 15,000 into rations for 23,000; rations for 8,000 then went unaccounted for over six months, and refugees received only a fraction of the aid.[22]

Stealing other assets related to relief operations is also a growth industry. In Burundi, Rwanda, Zaire, Uganda, Somalia, Ethiopia, and Sudan, militias have consistently looted cars and oil during emergency operations.

After years of watching the fight to contain diversion, one former regional director for an agency declares, "We can't reduce the diversion of food. It is a totally fungible resource. USAID (U.S. Agency for

International Development) can't tolerate this kind of talk. But we have to understand that food is an economic resource; it will be used in ways that suit the needs of authorities, no matter how tight you control the distribution process."[23]

Aid's Integration into Conflict Dynamics

Aid Increases Resources to Prosecute Conflicts

There are a number of ways in which aid inadvertently feeds conflicts by making more resources available to warring parties. Usually far less visible than overt diversion and looting, the following phenomena often contribute more to the financing of war and propping up of military authorities (governments, rebels, militias) than does the more visible stealing of food and drugs.

First, aid inputs are often "taxed" door to door, at distribution sites, or at markets. In some situations the figure is fixed, worked out over time between the community and the authority. In others, taxation is inconsistent, rising and falling in relation to the needs of the authority.

Second, extortion networks that include bribes, roadblocks, checkpoints, and Mafia protection rackets are common. Again, the security apparatuses that each agency constructed to protect its assets in Somalia are the extreme example, in which the demand for security buttressed the demand for weapons, fueling further cycles of rearmament beyond the internal warlord dynamic.

Third is the principle of fungibility, i.e., the substitution of international aid for local public welfare responsibilities, thus freeing resources for combat and often leading local populations to shift from productive activity to pursuing aid and in the process become more dependent and politically compliant.

Fourth, dual-currency exchange rates are hidden but huge. "All of these others are peanuts compared to the margins made in exchanging currency," says an agency representative. "It's the largest way of underwriting war efforts through aid." The late relief expert Fred Cuny once calculated that one rebel group that received foreign funds to do internal purchase placed what was in essence a 43 percent surcharge on their currency exchange. Such exchanges are often made in the Middle East.[24] Some governments charge up to four times the market rates and deposit the differences in their treasuries, thereby forcing donors who seek to reduce suffering to in fact subsidize continued oppression and violence by funding predatory regimes. Duffield notes that Sudan in 1988 restricted aid transactions to an official rate of 4.4 Sudanese pounds to 1 U.S. dollar while the parallel market rate was 17; Ethiopia in the 1980s charged roughly three times the market rate for Ethiopian birr.[25]

Fifth, rents, salaries (direct or taxed), fuel, transport contracts, and storage contracts are major sources of foreign currency for warleaders and their financiers. In Somalia, relief agencies could not help not only increasingly enriching the individual gunmen they employed but augmenting the ability of contractors and commanders to maintain militias—especially fleets of "technicals"—by controlling gunmen's access to aid work and thus loyalty.[26]

Sixth, import duties, licenses, permits, visas, and port or airport charges levied on humanitarian organizations and personnel are also large money-earners.

Seventh, local purchase schemes in which international agencies buy surplus commodities and transport them to deficit areas often provide foreign exchange to authorities or sometimes their private merchant supporters in surplus areas.

Eighth, the inclusion of warring authorities in assessments can sometimes facilitate their role as a pressure group for increased aid and can at times expose agencies to inaccurate assessment information because of incorrect translation or intimidation.

Ninth, in ignorance, aid inputs can help maintain black-market profiteering, in which merchant-militia or merchant-government alliances profit from controlled or manipulated scarcity and supply. Often these alliances will block aid to an area or withhold supplies from a market to drive prices up.

Tenth, aid provided to "indigenous" NGOs acting as fronts for military factions is yet another method for warleaders to accrue resources.

Finally, aid provided to third-party "security forces"—such as Zairian special forces hired by the UN to guarantee security in the Rwandan refugee camps—often goes straight into the pockets of corrupt military officials. As a result, in Goma extortion and theft from agencies are often simultaneously conducted by both the former Rwandan military and Zairian forces.[27]

"Humanitarian Infrastructures" Are Hijacked

The "humanitarian infrastructure" (the assets, agreements, and personnel that facilitate the delivery of aid) is often utilized by warring parties for purposes far different from those intended by aid providers. For example, human and physical assets are frequently conscripted in the war zone. Health workers, after receiving valuable training to prepare them to work with aid agencies, are conscripted into military service with depressing regularity. Agency vehicles and radios are "borrowed" and sometimes not returned. When they are stolen, militias sometimes even leave the agency logos on the vehicles to cover for their military operations, as has happened in Zaire. Building up the logistical capacity of a relief arm of a military authority inevitably builds the capacity of the authority itself.

Access agreements are often exploited to move military assets, as are aid modalities such as airstrips and roads. Airstrips are often used by military groups only hours after clearance has been given for relief flights to land, and flight routes into garrison towns that are part of negotiated access agreements allow these towns to be resupplied militarily. Roads that are built to facilitate the easier and cheaper movement of humanitarian supplies inevitably facilitate military movements as well.

Humanitarian cease-fires are frequently used by factions to redeploy and rearm while they bask in the congratulations from negotiators over their noble humanitarian gesture. The guinea-worm ceasefire in southern Sudan negotiated by former president Jimmy Carter in 1995 was a classic case of this manipulation of humanitarian intent: The government advanced its military aims by using proxies, such as the Ugandan Lord's Resistance Army and the West Nile Bank Front; a number of towns were taken by the government, including Pariang, Nasir, and Lafon; airstrips were mined, such as the one in Chotbura; and military assets were redeployed throughout the south by all sides.

Aid Exacerbates the Causes of War

Agencies usually focus—one project at a time—only on "communities" or "target groups" and can heighten tensions by ignoring the wider society as well as glossing over intracommunity conflicts of gender, class, or land rights. Major donors, similarly, can heighten conflict by widening gaps between the rich and poor or among resource competitors through economic aid or structural adjustment policies. The latter tend also to roll back a state's capacity and consequently its ability to mediate conflicts.[28] A description of some of the ways in which aid can undergird causes of conflict at the local level follows.

Aid Increases Competition

Aid can increase competition and suspicion in resource-scarce environments. Struggles to control relatively huge relief resources are critical to conflict *within* as well as *between* governments, rebel movements, and neighboring communities. This can happen when there is a perception of unbalanced aid, when targeting is disputed, or when access to aid is fought over.

Balance.   This increase in competition is especially true when there is a perception (accurate or not) of unbalanced aid provisioning to or agency placement in neighboring regions. Following the intercommunal clashes in Kenya's Rift Valley, there were charges and countercharges of partiality that fueled suspicions in an already tense environment. The perception of aid imbalances in favor of Rwandan refugee camps in Zaire and Tanzania has greatly angered the government in Kigali. Sudan is rife with examples: (1) When Norwegian People's Aid took aid to Didinga and Boya areas, bypassing Toposa areas, the Toposa threatened to stop all aid traffic until they were factored in; (2) perceptions by Jikany Nuer leaders of the disproportionate aid benefits accrued by Lau Nuer has helped fuel Jikany cattle raiding; and (3) larger perceptions of favoritism of Dinka areas over Nuer areas in the late 1980s and early 1990s fueled Nuer raids into Dinka areas following the split in the southern Sudanese rebel movement in 1991.

In Somalia, the United Nations Operation in Somalia (UNOSOM) contributed legendary imbalances to the Mogadishu economy with aid and contracts, continuously fueling conflict between subclan militias. Aid imbalances are constantly cited by Garhajis opposition forces in Somaliland as a fueling factor in their quest to overthrow the government; they claim that most aid assets went to serve populations displaced from government-held areas of the territory to the west, whereas little aid reached those displaced from opposition areas to the east until ICRC negotiated a more balanced response.

The multidonor evaluation of the response to the Rwandan emergency found that a large number of squatters have received aid in their new domiciles. "An unanticipated effect of seeds and tools distribution may be to entrench and appear to validate their hold on the land."[29] This result could lead to increased violence as refugee populations return and find their land taken over and aid agencies assisting the new occupants.

At the village level, there are many stories of the placement of a water well or health post sparking conflict between two communities. Not only can the location of a project spark conflict but as well whom an agency employs. In many zones of conflict, there are perceptions and misperceptions about the ethnic composition of those hired by agencies, and this problem in itself can fuel further fighting.

Aid can certainly draw armed elements to a relatively secure area, especially if surrounding areas perceive themselves as not being adequately served. In Somalia, "We don't want to tip regional balances by overconcentrating in stable areas," declares a diplomat. "Will that be potentially destabilizing and create a target?" For example, a hard analysis should be undertaken regarding to what degree the concentration of aid in Baidoa drew General Aidid's militia to that area in September 1995, beyond the obvious attraction of the grain harvest.[30] "Resources from the outside most certainly attract the vultures," says Ahmed Mumin Warfa, a Somali peace activist.[31] In southern Sudan, the local relief committee in Panthau told WFP not to bring in relief food because the community feared that it would draw a certain rebel commander (Kerobino) there, leading to inevitable plundering and asset-stripping. In the Masisi area of Zaire (north of Goma), Rwandan militia members have settled as refugees, exacerbating ethnic tensions and resulting in the burning and looting of villages.[32]

Targeting. Targeting—a desirable approach where possible—can inflame tensions when a surrounding community feels slighted. This perception can occur when agencies aid refugees and not host populations or attempt to target vulnerable populations rather than doing general distributions. Relief strategies should support local coping mechanisms, but with caution: Helping one group survive can burden another. Moving people from war to safety zones can support military depopulation strategies and lead to competition between displaced and host populations and local resentment of large-scale aid to displacees.[33] These situations are obviously exacerbated when there are identity differences between targeted and general populations, such as ethnicity, clan, religion, and so on. Targeting within societies, moreover, can exacerbate existing tensions because aiding the poorest of the poor, or women, necessarily entails repudiating and seeking to change the distributional status quo.[34]

For example, efforts to target WFP food to vulnerable groups in Kismayu, Somalia, got entangled with issues of payment of guards and led to perceptions within the city that aid was only going to certain segments of the community, eventually leading to violence in the WFP compound and the surrounding area. In Gursum, Ethiopia, Oromo displaced by intercommunal fighting in 1992–1993 were resettled in their former areas and targeted with grain, seeds, and tools. This targeting created great resentment in surrounding communities, and the distributions were physically prevented. Similarly, residents of Giseyni in Rwanda have attacked food trucks destined for refugees in Zaire, and Rwandan refugees in Tanzania have done the same to aid convoys passing them on the way to service the needs of refugees in Tanzania.[35]

Control of Aid or Access to Aid.   Manipulation or control of aid—or access to aid agency assets such as employment, contracts, and services—can become a source of conflict. "Large resource inputs create tensions," asserts one donor official. Macrae and Zwi stress that aid is not neutral but a political and economic resource often distributed, and thus manipulated and fought over, by the same groups initially responsible for violence and oppression—a process that sustains conflict and reinforces inequalities of power by heightening the current winners' power and wealth through their control of food.[36]

In southern Sudan, a partial cause for rebel factionalism is the desire to be a direct recipient of internationally provided aid as a "faction" controlling an area. After the first split in 1991, which OLS formally recognized fairly quickly, the consortium was much more careful in offering recognition to any new splinter groups.

In Somalia from 1991 through much of 1993, factions jostled to "capture" aid agency assets and employment, with some degree of success. The war in that country until mid-1991 was largely over resource control: camels, "technicals," food production, and fertile land. During the protracted war from late 1991 to the end of 1992, aid was the predominant liquid asset and a major resource in the country for anyone who controlled it. "Targeting of food aid by armed looters was largely devoid of any political motivation," says Geoffry Loane of ICRC. "The resources surrounding the humanitarian aid effort became the prime target."[37] Furthermore, Ken Menkhaus notes an "insidious impact of WFP's search for 'local NGOs' to distribute food in food-for-work projects. Ultimately, most of these organizations were fronts for local militias and politicians. This corrupts rather than strengthens local NGOs."[38]

Hiring, firing, and laying off of national staff in a complex emergency can lead to violence. Careful balance among clans in staff composition in Somalia, for example, is key in not provoking further conflict. Whom an agency rents from can create problems as well, especially because many agencies came to a place like Baidoa when General Aidid's forces were in control and were then left with rental contracts and staff from the occupying Habr Gedir community even after Aidid left in advance of the international intervention.

Aid Affects Authority Structures and Power Balances

Aid and distribution modalities can have a profound effect on the structure, quality, and balance of power in a community. Furthermore, provided in large tranches, aid can arguably impact the larger balance of power among warring parties.

Without participatory mechanisms and adroit management, aid can undermine traditional authority and social structures and capacities. Agencies must be very careful that their interventions do not prevent the growth of indigenous capacities or dwarf forms of social organization. "We constantly miss opportunities to strengthen traditional structures or support the building of new, better ones," laments a regional food-security advisor.[39] Furthermore, women are often undermined as primary providers for the household, although programming has dramatically improved in gender sensitivity in the past half-decade.

In a strong critique, Adams and Bradbury note that emergency relief programs often belie the supposed shift in development paradigms from technology- to people-centered, blueprint to process. Such programs are usually externally managed, nonparticipatory, and depend heavily on expatriate staff. They "intervene" to save "vulnerable groups" (often iconographed in Western appeals as helpless women and children) rather than "working with" "people" and developing local resources and skills. This situation reinforces the image and fact of dependency, which may serve aid bureaucracies' interests. To the extent that NGO aid shields indigenous leaders from responsibility and accountability, it further engenders dependency and intergroup tensions and can undermine cooperative relations.[40]

Agencies can undermine indigenous social structures and fledgling local authorities in zones of crisis by setting up parallel administrations resembling artificial economic islands in seas of little opportunity. On these islands, the best talent is employed for what is usually an externally framed set of priorities modeled after Western social welfare structures.

Inappropriately planned aid strategies can undermine local resilience and subsistence economies. Indigenous authorities and women usually have more of a stake than military authorities in preserving productive assets and livelihoods in the context of traditional community organization. When food aid is delivered (drawing military authorities) rather than animal health services, agricultural inputs, or fishing gear, the subsistence economy and indigenous social structure can be undermined. Vincent Coultan adds,

When people are in desperate need of immediate assistance, international interventions are appropriate and warmly welcomed. But the ability of many relief agencies to invest in locally sustainable "buffer capacity" is limited. Hierarchical direct emergency actions contribute to weakening indigenous resilience. The external relief organization often departs the scene with enhanced institutional memory exported within its expatriate staff and systems, whereas the client community can neither guarantee nor demand future access to those assets. The response decision is taken externally, often driven by relief fund availability and contracts spawned in the wake of the fleeting media circus spotlight. Additionally, agencies are often proudly protective of their right to independence of action and balk at being told where or where not to work, even if resources are not the primary constraint.[41]

Aid can also help create disincentives to traditional intercommunal cooperation or exchange networks if it addresses community needs divorced from their socioeconomic context, if it ignores historical trade patterns or exchange networks that respond to scarcity, or if it creates disincentives to endogenous production or migration responses to scarcity.

When the formation of refugee or internally displaced camps is encouraged for logistical or other reasons, it is important to note that these camps often can have a deleterious effect on traditional values and structures. In the large displaced camps in southern Sudan, "the sense of community has completely broken down," says Kevin Ashley, formerly of the World Food Program and now with Norwegian People's Aid. "Relief agencies are perpetuating this breakdown by not being creative."[42]

Perhaps the most overt impact of aid in its effect on authority is its potential to legitimize and thus strengthen warring parties. This result occurs when such parties claim credit for the provision of aid, mobilize populations on the basis of promised aid, organize or control local distribution structures, create differential provisioning to supporters and nonsupporters, participate in and agree to negotiated access processes, and underwrite "hearts and minds" campaigns. Warleaders usually seek to keep populations as dependent and politically compliant as possible. Political authorities' use of external aid to mobilize local populations increases both their legitimacy and populations' expectations of future aid. Aid can even have a negative effect when it is insufficient to satisfy food demands, but it acts as a magnet in displacing populations.[43]

The current effort by the Sudan government to bring OLS more tightly under its control is linked to the government's "peace from within" strategy. Linking the provision of aid, civil works, patronage, and other benefits of humanitarian assistance to itself is an integral part of the government's pacification campaign. Going beyond the normal liberties taken by governments, the Sudanese regime is deploying this comprehensive "peace from within" strategy in areas of significant opposition—armed and unarmed—and harassing, imprisoning, and executing those who don't comply. Even if it is only partially successful, the policy could have a major impact on the course of the war. In 1991, aid and recognition by OLS for the splinter faction of the SPLA undoubtedly kept that faction alive much longer than it would have survived under its own power. Agencies in the Rwandan refugee camps in Zaire—which for a long time were unwilling or unable to address the fact that they were also aiding the perpetrators of the genocide—did, over time, help to consolidate the authority of the genocide organizers within the camps.

Food aid dependency is often misunderstood as being primarily economic in nature. There is little evidence in the Horn to suggest that there is a widespread problem of local producers foolishly reducing production because of a reliance on low-quantity, intermittent food aid. "There is, however, evidence of producers not returning to production after a long period of food aid dependence," notes one longtime analyst. Politically motivated dependence can result when it is in the interest of authorities to maintain compliant populations in areas they control. Resource-poor areas can become dependent when political leaders use relief to mobilize local populations, as in Tigray during the Ethiopian civil war. Authorities can manipulate the response to the resulting need by lobbying aid agencies, leading the latter to make decisions in reaction to such advocacy pressures rather than objectively assessing needs.[44]

In Rwanda, distribution modalities that utilized former government structures—perhaps indispensable in the early stages of massive chaotic population movement—increasingly allowed for the reassertion of that authority's suzerainty in all areas of camp life as time went on. "Not only did these militia commanders control distribution," charges David Rieff, "but control over the food itself had become the source of their power and authority."[45] In Somalia, not only did the control of diverted food further empower certain militia leaders at the height of the civil war, but aid to the Marehan-dominated political structures (district councils) in Gedo Region endorsed and supported by UNOSOM, the United Nations Development Programme (UNDP), and the Life and Peace Institute legitimized the exclusion of Rahanweyne and Ogadeni populations from the authority structures of the region. In Ethiopia during the Derg, the government manipulated some aid agencies into inadvertently supporting its agenda of increasing its influence over the population in contested areas, especially in the context of its offensives during the 1984–1985 famine.[46] On the other side of the line, the Eritrean People's Liberation Front (EPLF) and Tigrayan People's Liberation Front (TPLF) used cross-border aid to underwrite their social mobilization strategies, in which reciprocity with civilian populations played a central role.[47]

An MSF report on the Rwandan refugee camps in Zaire notes the moral dilemmas posed by giving humanitarian relief in an unsustainable, militarized situation and by the open presence of refugees who allegedly committed genocide: "The debate is whether . . . to provide humanitarian assistance to a refugee population used by the perpetrators of the genocide as a means to increase their power . . . [or whether] in these circumstances it would be justified to cease the humanitarian assistance. . . . This debate has forced MSF to reconsider the boundaries of humanitarian aid."[48] The chaos of the Rwandan refugee flood into Zaire forced UNHCR and relief agencies to rely on those who presented themselves as leaders, many of whom had encouraged genocide.[49]

Military leaders are constantly having their authority legitimized by their participation in international conferences, negotiations, and other forums hosted or brokered by humanitarian agencies. When agencies and other outside bodies turn exclusively to warring parties when convening meetings, this situation undermines those segments of society that are working peacefully for alternatives.

These examples represent daily dilemmas faced by those responding in crisis—dilemmas that often have no clearly correct solutions. Ken Menkhaus concludes:

> When we [UNOSOM] attempted to broaden participation, we were accused of trying to marginalize these characters, and were blamed for their armed backlash! "Neutrality" with these social conflicts is impossible. Choices simply have to be made. The key is understanding and accepting the consequences of those choices.
>
> In the end, negative impacts resulting from our choices are simply unavoidable. *Any* introduction of assets will impact power relations, *any* interaction will tend to legitimize one group of leaders at another's expense. So then the challenge is simply to make astute choices.[50]

Aid Can Replace Local Responsibilities

Without appropriate engagement, aid can undermine or even replace the public welfare mandates of local authorities, thus encouraging them to pursue their war agendas unfettered by welfare responsibilities. "We're releasing authorities from their social contract," observes a donor official. This situation is attached to a broader phenomenon of the internationalization of public welfare responsibilities, as noted in detail by Mark Duffield. "The agencies come in like lifeguards," confirms an agency adviser.[51]

Not demanding accountability from local authorities (in the context of agreements on mutual accountability and responsibility) can have damaging effects on local welfare mandates. In southern Sudan, "some agencies have simply allowed certain percentages of their aid to be turned over to the military," asserts an agency head. This act reinforces the worst tendencies of predatory authorities, freeing them from any semblance of reciprocity with local populations. The more independent their supply lines are, the less authorities have to earn the trust and support of local populations. When the Rwandan Patriotic Front (RPF) launched its offensive in April 1994, a number of agencies followed it, assuming its social welfare responsibilities. "NGOs would go in front of each other to gain kudos from the RPF," relates one agency official. "This completely undermined the RPF's sense of responsibility." In Somaliland, "the ministries have no resources, so their tactic is to switch the responsibility to the agencies," charges Heywood Hadfield, former country director of Oxfam UK—Somalia.[52]

Mary Anderson makes the related point that aid providers who are or appear to be in solidarity with an authority's political or military objectives can harden the position of that authority and make it less likely to negotiate. Although an agency rarely explicitly endorses a political platform of an authority, informal contacts and unofficial relationships can have a tremendous impact on the authority's self-perception and choices. At other junctures, such solidarity may be appropriate, even necessary, as in the Nuba Mountains of Sudan or with Rwandan communities fleeing the genocide.[53]

3

Providing Aid Without Sustaining Conflict, Part One: Principles and Codes of Conduct

In order to pursue aid strategies that minimize the sustenance of conflict, there are a number of humanitarian principles and operational initiatives that should be considered. This chapter will examine two particular humanitarian principles—neutrality and accountability—for their relevance to minimizing conflict and then look at how codes of conduct can also contribute to reducing aid's contribution to violence. Chapter 4 looks at specific operational guidelines such as planning, monitoring, and coordination.

Before addressing the issue of principles, it is important to establish an overall aid framework that is conducive to minimizing the sustenance of conflict, and maximizing the contribution to community cohesion. Those constructing an overall framework for humanitarian aid that increases flexibility and is more relevant to complex emergencies should avoid the attempt to meet all possible basic needs (which is impossible anyway) but rather should attempt to help communities adapt to chronic crisis and manage change. This effort is best made through the restoration or protection of subsistence and through the building and supporting of indigenous capacity and community structures.

"The survival economy must be supported," says Abdi Aden Ali of Oxfam UK—Somalia. "Aid should help restore a survival system and expand survival capacity as soon as possible. The agencies should help continue what the community itself starts and owns."[1] Alex de Waal argues in a Sudanese case study that African communities' coping strategies aim more at ensuring the ability to resume future production when the crisis passes, by addressing factors that led to their present vulnerability, than at preventing present starvation. For example, communities in the 1984–1985 Darfur famine invested more in seeds and tools than in food.[2]

In trying to minimize aid's role in sustaining conflict or in build-

37

ing structures for peace, an individual project focus is inadequate. This critique is analogous to the women in development (WID) debate. WID projects can be marginally positive at the local level but are often structurally irrelevant. Similarly, the overall response context of humanitarian aid provision—including modalities and methodologies—must be examined because therein lies the vast majority of the inadvertent violations of the Hippocratic oath[3] ("First, Do No Harm") and the vast potential for peace building in the context of emergency operations. The devil, so to speak, is in the details, and anecdotes about interesting individual agency efforts are very difficult to transfer to other contexts when divorced from an overall strategic framework. "We need to be very attentive in the deployment of our resources," says Pierce Gerety, former country director of UNICEF—Somalia and current director of OLS. "We often don't look at distribution modalities and who they empower. In some places, avoiding trouble should be a major priority."[4]

To elaborate, it's very difficult to argue against the individual health clinic, hospital, or well project. But much emergency aid is an uncoordinated social welfare Band-Aid, and a very incomplete one at that. With limited resources (which may shrink further in relation to need), humanitarian assistance must be provided more strategically to address root causes: building civil structures, preventing famine, and reconciling local communities. Otherwise, we save the young child's life today only to have her face a dozen other possible deaths tomorrow.

The firm foundation upon which this more appropriate aid should be based is humanitarian principles, mostly rooted in the Geneva Conventions, the Convention on the Rights of the Child, and other relevant international humanitarian law. Larry Minear and Tom Weiss have cogently addressed the importance of humanitarian principles in their work.[5] Rather than marginally adding to their thorough treatment, only two principles will be addressed here, chosen for their relevance to the topic of minimizing the sustenance of conflict. The principles discussed—as well as others—should be disseminated widely and used to engage authorities and the communities in areas of their control on basic issues of accountability, reciprocity, and overall good governance.[6]

Rethinking Neutrality

One of the hottest debates in the field of humanitarian aid is the question of the appropriateness—and even the meaning of—neutrality.

The politicization of aid in conflict situations is a given. Nevertheless, the neutralist position might be summed up as follows: "The provision of humanitarian assistance should be made on the basis of need alone and should be above and beyond any political, military, strategic or sectarian agenda."[7] But the inevitable complications that attend traditional aid in complex emergencies—capture by factions, subversion by militias, legitimization of unsavory leaders, and fueling of competition—are encapsulated in the adage, "You may not take an interest in politics, but politics will always take an interest in you."[8]

Macrae and Zwi point out the ambiguities and dangers in the currently widespread humanitarian agency concept of "active neutrality," or giving both sides equal access to relief aid to enhance operational security, mitigate resource conflicts, and equally aid all civilians. Providing aid through indigenous relief agencies in rebel areas necessarily serves to politically legitimize their associated rebel organizations, who are thus able to feed the populations they seek to control. (The same could be said for governments and their relief agencies, such as Ethiopia's Relief and Rehabilitation Commission during the Mengistu regime.) More directly, such aid may sustain fighting forces and influence the dynamics of conflicts and the terms of settlements, as lack of access to aid may force rebels to accept a harsher peace. Even more troubling, organizations that attempt to give aid neutrally may support forces who harm the interest of and promote violence against civilian populations, such as RENAMO in Mozambique. An agency's alternative may well be to subject civilian populations to the double punishment of violence and hunger; however, it is clear that they must make such determinations case by case, not via a mechanical shibboleth of "neutrality."[9]

Most operational agencies claim to be neutral interveners but nonetheless acknowledge the inappropriateness or incompleteness of that concept. "No one regards NGOs as neutral anymore," says Andrew Natsios. "If you respond to need, you're helping the side that suffers more."[10] Angela Raven-Roberts of UNICEF affirms that NGOs and donors cannot avoid political issues by claiming neutrality.[11] In many complex emergencies marked by situations of divided governance, agencies find themselves painted as taking sides based on the geographical area or distribution modality they initially choose. (This problem is separate and distinct from aid's use as a geopolitical tool. "During the 1980s, humanitarian interventions were often related to the defeat of 'godless communism,'" recalls Willet Weeks.[12])

Duffield and Prendergast write,

> The evidence . . . shows that Western states and the UN still respond
> to complex emergencies by developing "neutral" institutions of
> humanitarian intervention which are then protected, if necessary, by
> military force. Enforcement is a difficult and vexed question; what
> we can insist on is that this change of emphasis has highlighted the
> political and structural nature of contemporary emergencies.
> "Neutral" intervention avoids engagement with the political reality
> it confronts. It eschews the need for supporting participatory and
> accountable structures and institutions, and arguably makes mat-
> ters worse.[13]

To avoid unfair allegations of partiality, agencies must be straightforward in their public statements. Again, transparency and openness are key. There is a responsibility to be vocal about violations of rights and principles, but great care must be taken to be predictable in condemning. Even in a situation in which agencies are feeding many of the perpetrators of Rwanda's genocide in refugee camps, some of the same agencies have worked publicly and privately to bring the killers to justice.

Rather than *neutrality,* which is a problematic term and does not accurately reflect the activities of many agencies and donors, a more appropriate term might be *independence,* or even *detachment.* Minear and Weiss prefer nonpartisanship over impartiality or neutrality. They define the nonpartisanship principle this way: "Humanitarian action responds to human suffering because people are in need, not to advance political, sectarian, or other extraneous agendas. It should not take sides in conflicts."[14] Stein Villumstad goes further, starting with the rejection of the concept of neutrality: "Norwegian Church Aid shares the following overall goal with the entire ecumenical network: 'give priority to measures which advance a more just distribution of goods and services, and ensure that the poorest benefit from them.' This is a highly political statement that involves human rights issues as well as power balance issues."[15]

One of the problems with neutrality is the trap of allowing balance objectives to take precedence over objective assessment. Another key humanitarian principle that needs to be continuously broadcast by humanitarian actors is that responding proportionally to need does not represent support for one side or another. Rather, it represents the right of agencies to independently assess humanitarian needs and respond commensurate to those needs, not in response to the inevitable political pressure to service particular areas disproportionately.

Nevertheless, there are times when the concept of balance does serve a purpose in the attempt to avoid igniting conflict. If an agency begins operating in one area and there are commensurate needs in another, all efforts should be expended to address those needs to prevent the perception of partiality. Such efforts require that agencies be knowledgeable of local political dynamics and intergroup relations. Agencies that claim an apolitical stance cannot be excused for ignoring such local dynamics; in such cases, ignorance can be deadly. Somalia is littered with nonfunctioning wells that weren't completed or rehabilitated because of conflict caused by perceptions of bias toward one group over another.

Similarly, it is incumbent on agencies to understand the local economic environment in which they are operating because ignoring it holds great potential for creating conflict. Knowing who owns the trucks in an area and being sensitive to who is contracted to service the logistical needs of an agency is critical in ensuring that perceptions are managed intelligently.

Sometimes the local dynamics shift so quickly that agencies are unable to obtain reliable information about what is actually going on in a particular location. In such cases (where war has not created a major humanitarian emergency), it may be best to do nothing but closely monitor the situation. For example, the resumption of civil war in Somaliland in late 1994 at times left many agencies uncertain about the reality in many areas. "Some agencies are not responding because of a fear of being accused of not being neutral," observes the country director of an NGO.[16] In this case, the Hippocratic oath might be best served by agencies staying on the sidelines, much to the chagrin of the warring factions.

As important as it is to understand local political and economic dynamics, many agencies feel that it is critical "not to get sucked into the political decision-making process," says Geoffry Loane. "We must retain the independence of aid."[17]

In Somaliland, most agencies that do have operations are concentrated in Hargeisa. This location has led to the inevitable charge of progovernment bias by the aid establishment. The problem would be rectifiable only if agencies decentralized operations by moving into all five regions of Somaliland, perhaps an economically unfeasible proposition.

Yet another complicating factor in the neutrality debate is the fact that human rights abuses are at the root of most emergencies that require a humanitarian response, and mandates of neutrality can conflict with the human rights advocacy necessary to address the causes of the suffering. In extreme cases, genocide goes on unchecked—as in Rwanda and Bosnia—while the international community provides humanitarian aid to survivors, allowing for some "political distance" between donors and the situations of slaughter to which they respond.[18] Francis Deng challenges the aid community by asking whether agencies can claim neutrality in the face of extreme oppression of a minority group and confine their response to emergency aid.[19]

There is obviously no panacea for the neutrality conundrum. Nevertheless, many agencies are initiating internal review processes to determine the most appropriate stance in given situations, and more attention is being paid to the debate by those within the aid community. The core of any agency policy should include the principles of independence and responding proportionately to need and should prioritize the gathering and analyzing of information on socioeconomic dynamics so that these principles can be carried out astutely.

Building Internal Accountability

A key objective of emergency operations should be the facilitation of a humanitarian lobby within the society receiving aid, strengthening internal mechanisms of accountability and internal demands for improved behavior by all parties in the aid relationship. Working through community structures can create an atmosphere in which the community itself demands a high degree of responsibility from those managing the program on its behalf. Information is key, as a study of Oxfam's emergency operations in East Africa concludes:

> Information puts people in a position of greater power. It builds systems of accountability to beneficiaries by telling them what they as individuals and as a community are entitled to receive. It gives them the knowledge with which to make a claim on those entitlements and to protect themselves from anyone who might try to deny them those entitlements. This is particularly important for women in cultures where information is shared between, and decisions taken by, men.
>
> There is overwhelming evidence from across East Africa that if people are aware of their entitlements, they are far less likely to be cheated or taken advantage of. . . .
>
> Everyone should know who is eligible to receive which items and (importantly) why. Entitlements should be read out in the local language at an open meeting before distribution.[20]

Operationally, transparency is critical for building internal accountability. Announcing to people what their ration is both publicly at the time of distribution and in advance through community structures provides a check on unimpeded diversions by rapacious authorities—whether military, commercial, or civil. Even where civilian voices are subordinate to the military, this information can create an opening for communal demands for each person's "fair share." This social pressure is critical, and likely much more important than outsiders' demands. "Society itself is the most important policing mechanism," states a USAID field staffer. In southern Sudan, "the SPLA has introduced a culture of suspicion and intimidation," says a southern Sudanese employee of an NGO. "The tradition is that people challenge each other, and that tradition can be tapped."

In the Rwandan refugee camps in Zaire, what initially had been brute intimidation of refugees by camp leaders gave way to intimidation based on misinformation. This analysis by some agencies led to a mass information campaign to empower refugees to make their own choices to the maximum extent possible. UNHCR initiated radio broadcasts to highlight secure returnee communities. This approach undercuts the camp leaders' rule by terror based on misinformation.

In the Ngara refugee camp in Tanzania, ICRC personnel obtained megaphones, gathered the masses before distributions, and explained exactly what people were entitled to and the process. An observer of the process describes it this way: "First they made people understand what they deserved. Then they went to the responsibles and told them what they should do. That way the people couldn't come back and say that they were cheated."

In southern Sudan, the rationale for the establishment of relief committees by local churches and later by WFP was that ultimately local communities play the most important role in making the SPLA accountable for aid distributions. Individual NGOs have reached this conclusion as well. One NGO, for example, distributes its aid based on the decisions made at public meetings of the chiefs, subchiefs, and *gol* leaders. "The SPLA will inevitably get fed. They are part of the community. Accountability must be demanded by the people," says the agency's country director.

External conditions requiring accountability can reinforce internal demands for the same. Accountability means not only responsibly managing resources but also articulating and applying principles.

Timing of aid deliveries and distributions is also important in minimizing the ease of diversion. For example, when food is delivered during harvest time, communities often have less interest in protecting their rights to the assistance because they are preoccupied with their own production and exchange. Yet distributions frequently coincide with harvests despite decades of such damaging evidence.

Finally, accountability needs to be a two-way street. According to an African Rights paper, aid agencies are "less assiduous about providing relevant information, or making definite commitments, to the people whom they are supposed to be serving; the donor populations and the intended beneficiary populations." The organization suggests that two-way accountability can be enforced only through a system of legal redress, "backed by proper judicial procedures. . . . For the requirements of aid in southern Sudan it would be necessary to develop the indigenous legal system, or to set up special tribunals."[21]

Operationalizing Principles: International Codes of Conduct

Numerous attempts have been made to establish a basic set of principles that might guide humanitarian action. A number of agencies, responding to the impact of aid in disasters and conflicts, have established the International Red Cross/Red Crescent and NGO Code of Conduct to introduce some measure of regulation of disaster assistance.[22] Given the diversity among relief organizations, developing separate codes of conduct for similar groups might be more practical than attempting to devise an all-purpose code.[23] Nevertheless, if the number of NGOs responding to emergencies continues to rise rapidly, perhaps a mandatory set of regulations and an audit system should be introduced by donor countries in partnership with affected countries.

Some agency representatives support unanimity. "A code of conduct would be extremely positive as a generally accepted tool or guideline for operations if it has unanimous support," says Geoffry Loane of ICRC. "It should be kept very simple, and should be used as a guide and a way of harmonizing the activities of all actors."[24] A Rwandan official concurs: "The best enforcement mechanism for a code of conduct is good example."[25] Furthermore, humanitarian principles "can help make war slightly less brutal; they can reinject a sense of fair play," says an NGO's regional adviser.[26]

In the attempt to reduce diversion, both a firm commitment to basic principles and wide dissemination of these principles are needed. To the greatest extent possible, the principles should be mutually agreed upon by aid providers and various recipient constituencies, both military and civil. "Ground rules are a tool for communication," says Helge Rohn of Norwegian People's Aid.[27] "Ground rules are critical," confirms Kevin Ashley. "Some kind of contract is needed.

Many people in relief are not professionals, yet they are the frontline diplomats."[28]

In some contexts, a unique code may be required, but there is often a lack of respect for existing international legal principles. "We can't go in at the outset of every emergency and renegotiate new terms of reference," points out Loane.[29] Adherence to existing or negotiated codes can be used as a yardstick for the international acceptance of the legitimacy of an authority. This positive form of conditionality can provide a lever for behavioral change on the part of abusive and predatory authorities. There is also much room to do principle building before a crisis erupts rather than waiting for the eruption and then introducing codes, ground rules, or conventions.

There is a pressing need in many complex emergencies to stop the cycle of impunity regarding abuse of humanitarian intent. "Principles aren't much use without a historical context," warns anthropologist John Ryle. "There is no incident book in most situations; no one agrees on what's happened. Patterns of looting are obscured."[30] Once ground rules are introduced, enforcement must be evenhanded and agencies must stand firm from the outset, especially with regard to freedom of movement and independence of operations in the quest for safe humanitarian space.

Among NGOs, UN agencies, and donors, there is an increasing "recognition of the need for an institutional response to security incidents," proclaims a UN Department of Humanitarian Affairs (DHA) concept paper. "Protagonists are to be held directly accountable to the UN and the international community for attacks on UN staff and others connected with UN humanitarian operations and also for denial of access and diversion of aid."[31] If agencies are publicly to address the issue of diversion and abuse, all must do so openly; collectively; and through detailed, public chronicling of incidents rather than glossing over major diversions and providing further relief to replace looted provisions.[32] Sudanese local churches have shown that urging warring parties to honor humanitarian principles and alerting them to the consequences in bad publicity of their failure to do so can go hand in hand.[33]

There is growing discussion about the need to be able to stop aid in response to the abuse of humanitarian principles. Suspension of aid is much more logical in the context of a framework of agreement between parties about minimal operating conditions. A clear distinction must be drawn between suspending operations in a difficult context and complete withdrawal. The former allows more flexibility in negotiation as well as keeping open the option of maintaining a witnessing function. The latter represents an option of last resort, only invoked when it becomes apparent that the aid and relief organization presence do more harm than good. (For more information on this issue, see Chapter 6.)

One danger of codes of conduct is their vulnerability to political manipulation. Codes (and resulting sanctions) can be invoked for subjective reasons and can create dilemmas and interruptions in resource-scarce, volatile regions marked by divided authority and mixed front lines. Transparent procedures for utilizing the codes would be a critical prerequisite for their deployment in a conflict situation.

Another potential minefield is how to include rebel movements in ground-rule signing and dissemination. "You'll have major problems with governments," predicts an agency representative. More broadly, many program managers in the field expressed skepticism about the acceptability to governments of codes of conduct, believing that the relevance of such codes is confined to situations of disputed, divided, or unclear authority.

Yet another problem with codes and ground rules is that they often ignore traditional legal principles inherent in an affected society. Additional efforts must be undertaken to make international principles relevant in the context of what are often richly developed indigenous principles of group interaction and justice.

A fourth obstacle is the difficulty inherent in coordinating all (or even some) of the agencies responding to an emergency in their implementation of any particular code. "There are always external influences which might override in-country agreement," observes the former country director of an NGO in Rwanda. Coordination was a major problem in Rwanda, where 150 NGOs descended on the postgenocide emergency with remarkable differences in professional standards. "Without some basic code, what is an NGO?" asks the country director of another NGO in Kigali. "We are losing our special status."

On the subject of implementation of principles, Bradbury offers an interesting suggestion: "Donors should consider ways to translate the codes into guidelines that will inform the allocation of funds to implementing agencies. This will require donors and multilateral agencies to take a proactive role in supporting those national governments who legitimately wish to regulate NGOs."[34]

A major difficulty arises in the identification and definition of appropriate principles. In the ratcheting up of a response to a complex emergency, agencies and donors should coordinate efforts to develop a joint set of ground rules upon which to base their response. The Geneva Conventions are the foundation, but often specific situations require unique adaptations of existing principles. The search for appropriate responses should be made as consultative as possible and should include armed and unarmed groups from the affected country.

Ultimately, moving toward some form of international accreditation system is most desirable. Particular adaptations for specific contexts would utilize a basic code as a starting point. Any such code should be developed in full partnership with international and local humanitarian actors. If no overall accreditation system can be agreed upon, increased regulation could be an intermediate option, including the restriction of donor funding and preferential tax treatment to signatories of the code and host country restrictions on nonsignatory agencies.[35]

Case Examples

For years the ICRC has made the dissemination of the Geneva Conventions to warring parties and abusive authorities a priority. In certain regions in one particular country in the Horn—plagued by low-intensity conflict between the government and a number of rebel militias—numerous observers on the ground have pointed out that the ICRC's quiet dissemination has had a positive effect.

Outside the Greater Horn, in the former Yugoslavia, one of the main activities of UNICEF has been the promotion of the Convention on the Rights of the Child. The convention was translated into all languages of the region and disseminated widely, especially to rank-and-file soldiers at checkpoints. Numerous UNICEF staff in the Greater Horn are interested in pursuing this activity in their programming.

In Rwanda, some aid agencies are attempting to promote the Convention on the Rights of the Child in group and family contexts rather than in its application to the individual. Members have rights in groups, and children have rights (and responsibilities) in families.

Individual NGOs often have their own internal ground rules. In Akon, southern Sudan, the SPLA commandeered cars and other assets from SCF—UK, which decided to pull out (despite a huge investment) and bring a case against the SPLA in the traditional chiefs' court in the town.

A group of NGOs in southern Sudan has developed a set of conditionalities parallel to the OLS ground-rule process in order to present a common NGO stance on (and response to) the abuses of humanitarian assistance. Initial discussions regarding conditions emphasized the need for independent access, monitoring, and assessment.

In this NGO framework, human rights are prominently included along with humanitarian principles. Violations against local Sudanese civilian populations are addressed as well as abuses against agency personnel and assets. "Up until now, there's been a total neglect of the rights of ordinary people of south Sudan," says Philip Winter, former head of SCF—UK's program in southern Sudan. "But we will not be advocating human rights to beat the heads of the rebel factions. The NGOs are more concerned with practical rights—food, security, and school opportunities."[36]

Discussion is under way within UNICEF about the need for a Division of Protection such as that which UNHCR already has. "There is plenty of emergency and development expertise," says one OLS official. "We need guidance and analysis on protection. Child labor, prostitution, and imprisonment should be addressed in addition to the war-related issues."[37]

Beyond current ground-rule initiatives, field staff (both local and international) constantly toy with ideas on how to address egregious violations of principles in their areas of operation. For example, animal health services are an extremely valued *economic* as well as humanitarian input in pastoral settings during war. Often intercommunal livestock raiding is rampant, heightened by the impunity afforded by the breakdown of judicial processes accompanying a complex emergency. Tim Leyland, a veteran of animal health interventions, offered this proposal:

> Livestock programmers need to go into particular communities and talk about issues of raiding. Let the community itself lay down the ground rules, especially regarding raiding. We should be going in up front and asking them what they would do to ensure a good operating environment. During this community dialogue process, the agencies should introduce certain principles and the idea that we have the right to withdraw inputs if these principles are abused.[38]

Both Somalia and Sudan are the subjects of experiments in applied humanitarian principles. The Somalia Aid Coordination Body (SACB)—the donor coordination group—introduced a Code of Conduct, and the OLS's Humanitarian Principles section negotiated an agreement on ground rules that was recently signed by the two larger rebel factions. As resources become tighter, donors will inevitably express increasing interest in creative approaches to the abuse of humanitarian principles.

Somalia Code of Conduct

The SACB's Code of Conduct, established in early 1995, prioritizes the establishment of secure and less intrusive (freedom of program implementation, hiring and discharging personnel, etc.) conditions for aid agencies as prerequisites for their provision of nonemergency aid.

When aid worker Rudy Marq from AICF was kidnapped in January 1995, the SACB scaled down quickly to emergency-only operations, suspending all rehabilitative or developmental activities. Community pressure on the kidnappers helped lead to Marq's eventual release. Later, when the Supreme Governing Council in Baidoa wanted to dictate whom agencies would hire and fire, the code was invoked to protect agencies from undue interference.

Questions have arisen regarding the code's approach. Somali critics say that the process was unilateral and heavy-handed, not consultative. "The approach needs to be different," notes a high-ranking UN official. Another aid consultant concurred: "The code needed to be more consultative, more of a partnership. The presentation is the problem, not the content." Even some donors are uneasy with the arrangement, as one donor official summarizes: "The code is very patronizing; it is not a mutual contract." The code is open to wide interpretation by various donors. Certain phrases—such as *secure regions*—are not clearly defined. No mechanism of enforcement existed at the outset, nor any common formula for responses to violations.

These problems lead to the code being arbitrarily applied. A series of mistakes made by WFP staff compounded a difficult situation involving a WFP warehouse, security guards, and a Somali general in Kismayu. Operations were scaled back to emergency-only, despite the shared culpability for the dispute and the need to expand information gathering on deteriorating nutritional conditions in the Juba Valley and Kismayu itself.

Another critique revolves around the issue of how representative local authorities area. The SACB went on a field mission to Gedo Region and found that the authorities had met its conditions for assistance, which are heavily weighted toward the stability and security of international agencies. When the "authorities" of the community accepted the code, the mission officials recommended the commencement of rehabilitation and reconstruction activities in the region. But the authorities in the region are almost exclusively from one subclan (Marehan), whereas Ogadeni and Rahanweyne, who make up a substantial percentage of the region's population, are almost completely unrepresented. "Justice has been sacrificed at the mantle of stability," laments one Somali official.

Yet another issue with the code is the demand that individual perpetrators be punished for crimes against agencies. This approach is problematic in the current context of no justice system and the historical context in which groups negotiate compensation in lieu of individual punishment.

One debate to which the Somali experience will contribute is the prerequisite of security for undertaking rehabilitative initiatives. Is it possible for "authorities" to guarantee security? Which authorities should be recognized? Does providing aid to secure areas and ignoring insecure ones draw predators to the secure areas? Did this last factor contribute to Aidid's invasion of Baidoa? Careful study of the response to the Somali code will provide important answers.

Sudan Ground Rules

In Sudan, the OLS-brokered ground rules include the following central points: The protection of civilians is fundamental to aid delivery; civilians have a right to live in safety and dignity; aid cannot be denied even if it crosses lines of battle; responding proportionately to need does not represent an abandonment of neutrality; and transparency of operations will be followed at all times.

The southern Sudan ground rules have been signed by OLS and the two major rebel factions in the south. It is the first time anywhere in the world that rebel organizations have recognized and signed the Convention on the Rights of the Child. Others (Palestine Liberation Organization, Tamil Tigers) have signed the Geneva Conventions. The OLS ground rules also stress protection of civilians as an integral part of assistance. The Geneva Conventions and the Convention on the Rights of the Child undergird the ground rules. Urging greater respect for human rights is very palpably encouraging greater democratization and better governance. "The violence and predation must be opposed," asserts an aid official. "We are helping people to rethink the way they're waging war."

Two or three months before the August 1995 signing of the ground rules, there were four significant violations of humanitarian operations. "OLS cut off the tap" in all cases, says a relief official based in southern Sudan. "Four commanders are in the process of being transferred."[39] A former NGO country director, Philip Winter, notes, "Finally, NGOs are starting to withdraw aid when there are serious abuses of principles."[40] However, African Rights notes that this response did not include specific agreement on how to prevent such incidents in the future. "Aid diversions have been systematic in the past, and there is no particular reason to believe that they will be less a part of the dynamic of war in the future," concludes an African Rights report.[41] But this conclusion is premature, and a sequel to the report is necessary to assess the effect of initiatives such as the ground rules and relief committees.

After the signing of the ground rules by the rebel factions, the first major violation involved a revenge attack by an Akot-based group of civilians and SPLA soldiers on SSIA-held villages in the Ganliel area of Western Upper Nile in which 210 civilians were allegedly killed, including 127 children. OLS officials immediately met with the Sudan Relief and Rehabilitation Association (SRRA) leaders, using the ground rules as the basis for discussion. OLS and the SRRA agreed upon the following measures: an inquiry and disciplinary actions against SPLA or SRRA officials; the necessity of locating and returning missing children; the holding of the first ground-rules dissemination exercise in the Akot area, especially for commanders; and the need for grassroots peace and reconciliation activities by the chiefs of both areas.

In Mundri County in early 1996, agencies shut down their operations servicing the needs of about 12,750 displaced persons because of problems with local authorities. Although the hardships experienced by the displaced undoubtedly increased, a large number began to move back to their home areas, seeking assistance from relatives and improving their chances of long-term self-reliance, given some measure of security.[42]

A major shortcoming of the southern Sudan ground rules is that they have only been offered to and signed by the rebel factions. A corresponding interest on the part of the leaders of OLS in Khartoum is not there. This problem leaves agencies open to charges of double standards because they appear to be placing higher demands and expectations on rebels than on the government. African Rights points out another problem with the ground rules:

> Instead of a contract or ultimatum stating the minimum conditions under which aid agencies could do their work, the Ground Rules became an educational document for building civil society in South Sudan.
> This change made some sense. It may not be possible for groups of aid agencies to set minimum conditions, and stick to them in solidarity with one another. But by abandoning the attempt, they greatly weaken their ability to control—and understand the effects of—their own programs. They become less genuinely accountable to their donors.[43]

In this regard, the most important drawback to the ground rules is the lack of any enforcement mechanism for major violations by any party, including the donors. Processes are spelled out, but in the end no real sanctions are available.

4

Providing Aid Without Sustaining Conflict, Part Two: Ten Commandments

Aid can help sustain conflict—or a party to a conflict—as a function of policy. But, as highlighted in Chapter 2, humanitarian assistance also inadvertently feeds conflict. When addressing the latter phenomenon, in order to minimize fueling the fire, operational approaches need to be reevaluated and reoriented. As a start, Macrae and Zwi advise aid organizations to increase their accountability by including beneficiaries in planning, more accurately analyzing local politics and assessing local organizations' capacities and limits, and supporting indigenous humanitarian agencies where they can deliver relief and help rebuild shattered societies.[1]

At a 1995 seminar on aid and conflict organized by David Smock and the U.S. Institute of Peace, Peter Shiras of InterAction pointed out, "We need to distinguish between those factors we can influence and those we cannot, and then look at ways in which we can really minimize the factors we can affect, like theft and taxation."[2]

There are ten aspects of humanitarian aid operations that—if reoriented—hold the potential for minimizing harmful conflict-sustaining side effects. These ten commandments are: deepen analysis in planning and diversify information sources; properly and independently assess needs; study options for modalities of access; be astute and flexible in the types of aid provided; study impacts of targeting and distribution methods; standardize costs and minimize extortion and hyperinflation; commit to independent monitoring and evaluation; integrate human rights monitoring, advocacy, and capacity-building objectives; coordinate at all levels; and prioritize engagement and capacity building with authorities and civil institutions.

Commandment 1: Deepen Analysis in Planning and Diversify Information Sources

Poor or shortsighted planning at the outset of an emergency response can dictate to a great degree the extent to which negative impacts result from that response. Questions about the effect of conflict on aid operations and the effect of aid operations on conflict need to be dealt with at the planning stage. Relief planners must broaden the scope of their attention, Keen and Wilson argue, from how operations reach at-risk persons to how they affect the economic and military strategies of all parties—those who suffer directly or indirectly and those who can alleviate, benefit from, or help to create famine and displacement. Planners must think in terms not of commodities but of winners and losers.[3]

In the Rwandan camps, for example, "humanitarian need was the imperative, but thinking strategically about repatriation from the beginning was lacking," says a donor representative. "There was never pressure from the UN system to plan in terms of a regional response." Jeff Drumtra of the U.S. Committee for Refugees calls the information disconnect between NGOs operating in the refugee camps and the NGOs inside Rwanda the "Iron Curtain."[4]

Macrae and Zwi urge that community-level project planners take explicit account of the risk that unequal development patterns and relief inputs will intensify existing ethnic or religious tensions into violence in communities under enviro-economic stress, citing the examples of northern Somalia and southern Sudan.[5]

Planning for appropriate timing of a response can be key. Providing food aid during harvest time, a hallmark of nearly every haphazard emergency response, results in less interest in the aid on the part of the local community and thus an easier target for diversion by warring parties. Timing in the provision of inputs other than food is obviously critical as well. In Rwanda in 1995, the Food and Agriculture Organization (FAO) called for a meeting on seed distribution roughly one month before the rains were to begin. This lack of planning indirectly hinders broader objectives of facilitating refugee repatriation, a prerequisite for any reconciliation process. How can refugees be confident about returning if the assistance infrastructure is not in place?

One way to encourage better agency planning is to build more extensive guidelines and requirements into requests for proposals (RFPs). There is a wide disparity between what different donors require in proposals they solicit (as well as a wide variation in quality of planning among the agencies). "Well-designed donor guidelines and requirements on grant proposals will force agencies into better planning," says Helge Rohn of Norwegian People's Aid.[6] Another donor official concurs: "There is a core of NGOs and UN agencies which are very good, and lots that are rubbish. Donors need to be more responsible in asking questions." Demonstrating that agencies do indeed have a short- and medium-term plan of action should be a minimal requirement of funding, to maximize sustainability and operational integrity. Mechanisms to exclude those that don't meet minimal guidelines should be explored.

Part of the planning nexus is having the appropriate personnel available. Aid workers frequently cite the one variable that distinguishes politically adroit operations from business-as-usual: the quality of personnel. "We need a 'first team' of sophisticated operators to deal with the Rwandas and Somalias when they erupt," says another donor official. UNICEF has moved in this direction by creating a global Rapid Response Team, and NGOs such as CARE are looking at ways to preposition experienced personnel in situations deemed likely to explode. CARE is currently developing a contingency plan for the Greater Horn with an investment of about $2 million. It will be a test case for this kind of NGO planning. In waiting for the eruption in slow-onset emergencies, agencies lose opportunities to employ experience and information, which are critical in minimizing the negative externalities of aid.

Advanced planning plays a central role in crisis prevention. "We need to do dress rehearsals and simulations to deal with diversion and violence," recommends a donor official. For example, the official continues, "Our training in Somalia didn't deal with political issues or negotiating with faction leaders. Field staff never saw any clan trees or had any basic political or social briefings." To rectify this, Burundi (and the Great Lakes Region) has been the subject of a number of advanced planning exercises by several donor and operational agencies. The U.S. Office of Foreign Disaster Assistance (OFDA) has identified a potential Disaster Assistance Response Team (DART) in case of a major surge in violence and consequent humanitarian need, although that team has not had any Burundi-specific training or preparation. The earlier and better-prepared the response, the earlier rehabilitative principles can be introduced into the aid package and the sooner the minimization of aid's sustenance of conflict can be addressed.

Donor countries need to have updated plans of action for areas that threaten to erupt. "Both the State [Department] and U.S. Agency for International Development Inspector Generals consistently remark on the lack of mission preparation with specific reference to Mission Disaster Relief Plans and Emergency Action Plans," points out a cable addressing U.S. disaster assistance.[7]

Planning for relevant community participation is a major determinant in building internal community accountability. The chain of inconsistent accountability referred to in Chapter 1 begins with poor planning, and war economies are often reinforced as a result. The traumatic disempowerment that low-intensity military tactics impose on many groups, such as women, makes it vital to ensure broad local participation in, and reempowerment through, rehabilitation planning.[8]

Planning should also strive to minimize dislocation of populations. A displaced population and the aid it receives are more vulnerable to manipulation by military leaders. OFDA's DART team in northern Iraq was key in developing the plan to resettle displaced Kurds back in their home areas rather than in the mountain camps in which the U.S. military was prepared to continue a major operation to feed them.

Many agencies need guidance regarding the local context in which they operate. There is often little understanding of aid's impact on conflict or its potential for reconciliation. In some cases, this problem can be rectified by making already produced information available to agency staff. Analysis of the military situation needs to be made available to agency personnel, both policymakers and implementers. Key literature on sectoral or programming priorities would also be necessary, such as information on capacity-building techniques and results. Efforts should be made to preserve institutional memory by making situation reports accessible to present as well as future staff and to share these reports to the greatest extent possible among agencies. For example, after being in existence for six years, OLS is developing a resource center in Lokichoggio, Kenya, the location from which most agency personnel (and others) travel to southern Sudan.

In other cases, either the literature is insufficient or the situation is so fluid that most written information is inadequate. In that event, it may be advisable for an agency or a consortium of agencies to hire a country expert on a short-term basis, someone who is aware of intercommunal dynamics and political and economic realities and who can advise agencies on hiring practices and aid activities that might minimize the contribution of these actions to the escalation of conflict. "In the early stages, someone with cultural insights would be just invaluable," asserts a field contractor in Rwanda. "This tends to be the weak link in our response, and a clash of values often results." Another field staffer concurs, suggesting that emergency response teams should include "someone to provide insights into the sociology of culture."

For example, many agencies responding to the mass exodus of Rwandans to Zaire and Tanzania were not fully aware of the political structures that were quickly being reconstituted in the camps. Similarly, the emphasis of the intervention of the United Task Force (Somalia) (UNITAF) in Somalia was also partly based on misanalysis of information, and the agencies that preceded UNITAF had huge differences in their level of understanding of the local dynamics of the areas in which they were involved. "Most problems where emergencies become chronic and agencies are unable to disengage usually stem from misinterpretations in the first place," says Willet Weeks.[9]

Ioan Lewis of the London School of Economics points out that the field representatives of the colonial powers were "much better equipped professionally than the new missionaries in the NGOs." He suggests that much more systematic training and briefing should be provided for current aid workers.[10]

At the aforementioned U.S. Institute of Peace roundtable, Russ Kerr of World Vision highlighted the confusion resulting from complex emergencies. He urged NGOs to expand their information sharing in order to better ascertain political agendas, military dynamics, and the level of support enjoyed by authorities.[11] The multidonor evaluation of the response to the Rwandan emergency found that there was no "mechanism for monitoring and analyzing information to provide warning of population movements" that was usable.[12]

Besides making information available to agency personnel, there is a critical need to set aside "programming time to read, analyze, and discuss this important socioeconomic-political-cultural information pertaining to the crisis at hand," suggests a donor agency veteran. "This education process needs to be seen as just as important as the 'doing' in an initial emergency response."

Having ethnographic or sociological expertise within an agency can assist that agency in developing population profiles of communities *before* an emergency erupts. Risk-mapping, with all of the various ingredients, can make emergency response much more efficient and reduce mistakes that help sustain conflict. Throughout the response to a complex emergency, the development of a solid information system is critical. In the case of Somalia in mid-1995, according to Walid Musa of the UN Coordination Unit in Somalia, "The information system is the strategy."[13]

The quality of information is also an issue. Agency reports are usually the primary source of information for policymakers and donors in chronic conflict areas. What the information is being used for—fund-raising, resource deployment, public education—has a bearing on what information is presented and how it is presented. Often agency responses are glorified as having saved thousands from the jaws of starvation and anarchy, and there are few alternative sources of information to challenge this view. Furthermore, little thought is given to how to "disseminate information that will assist the victims and impede those who exacerbate or profit from disaster."[14]

Regarding managerial matters, the newly created UNICEF Rapid Response Team is discussing the feasibility of bringing in an internal auditor within one month of the onset of an emergency operation to evaluate the aid effort and advise the agency on how to avoid major mistakes. The operations director of a U.S. NGO agrees with this need: "[Early on], someone needs to come in at the management level and ask basic implementation questions. A common set of questions ought to be developed for all agencies."

"Previous or ongoing involvement in development work should help inform planning for potential emergencies," notes one analyst. "If an agency is operating now in Uganda in a 'development mode,' an important planning element is preparation for potential impacts of renewed conflict or a major refugee influx."

Commandment 2: Assess Needs Properly and Independently

One of the principal culprits in creating an environment for easy diversion of aid is the inflation of population figures, a result of poor or inadequate assessment. (This problem is of course compounded by the lack of accurate census data in most African countries to begin with.) The proper collection of data is critical, especially in situations of mass concentrations of refugees or internally displaced people. Insufficient or simplistic assessments—especially those that don't properly factor in the effect of conflict on local economies—are another weak link in the aforementioned chain of inconsistent accountability.

Another cause of aid feeding conflict is that assessments usually do not uncover the entire food economy, especially the unofficial markets that are created by stolen commodities. These economic channels need to be understood. Where do the commodities go? Who sells them? Who gets the money? Who else benefits? Agencies must work out the hidden links. "In order to do this, we need to refrain from humanitarian thinking," says an agency veteran.

Decisions that agencies make about the deployment and utilization of resources can have profound impacts on economies and power structures. Ignorance of these structures—even when resulting from a misguided sense of do-good neutrality—is inexcusable.

Assessment models that don't uncover these economic circles are inadequate for war situations. Kathi Austin highlights the repercussions in Zaire:

> Aid can cause immense distortions and fluctuations in the local currency, commodity prices, and the inflation rate. In Bukavu [Zaire], for example, local peoples were forced to vacate residences they were renting when the refugees came in and could offer to pay higher rents. Local bars, restaurants, and shops also closed because they could not often compete with those set up by refugees who had pilfered aid supplies and were now selling these cheaply. The conflict created over these disparities, in part, has led the local Zairian population and its authorities to push for a quick return home of the Rwandan refugees—even if this means forced repatriation.
>
> In eastern Zaire, resold aid supplies provided the coffers from which the former Rwandan government has purchased weapons, ammunition, and fuel for military transport.[15]

Average or general pictures are meaningless in emergencies: Broad nutritional surveys, if possible, would be uninformative and mask or hide the localized crises that make up emergencies. Nutritionists Helen Young and Susanne Jaspars thus support "sentinel site" monitoring of a few selected communities—complemented by rapid assessment capacity—as saving personnel, costs, and time and facilitating rapport with local people and subtle analysis and differentiation of groups. But Young and Jaspars question the foundations on which current assessment techniques rest:

> The discipline of nutrition as it is currently applied is rapidly becoming irrelevant to the problems of famine-affected populations and refugees. . . . We have been seduced by anthropometry, which is easy to measure, easy to manipulate and can be easily taken out of context to mean just about anything! This has stunted our analytical skills, and created a strait-jacketed approach to famine relief; high rates of malnutrition equal famine equal food distribution.[16]

A critical question that assessments must answer is why people are vulnerable; that is, what are the multiple factors that cause a food system to break down or cause a rapid deterioration of the health of people in a community? Needs assessments must address the totality of human needs, problems, and capacities.

One attempt to ask not just why people are dying but also how they survive has been the food economy assessment model, introduced by OLS in southern Sudan with the institutional help of SCF—UK. OLS has experimented with its assessment techniques, striving to combine quantitative and qualitative data. Whereas 1992–1993 assessments focused on quantitative, household-level data, placing wider socioeconomic and military issues in the background, the 1994 assessments introduced the food economy approach, derived from SCF—UK work on risk-mapping in food crises. This approach measures and ranks the degree of potential food deficit in caloric terms among different population subgroups, allowing agencies to target the acutely vulnerable. Researchers ask key informants (usually household members, which allows assessment teams to bypass military authorities) to estimate the foods available to the "average household" in the population; then they calculate and pie-chart the percentage shortfall in households' energy needs.[17] The focus on available-food-converted-into-energy derives from classic household food consumption study techniques; by using key informants rather than household surveys, researchers can extend this costly approach to emergency needs assessment.[18]

"With the food economy model, we have a rationalization of why we do or do not help in a given situation," says Kevin Ashley. "We have a mandate."[19] "The food economy model has reduced overt diversion in southern Sudan simply by making it harder to divert," asserts another agency field officer.[20]

On the other hand, there are critiques of the conceptual underpinnings of the food economy approach to emergency need assessment, which derives from Amartya Sen's entitlement theory that famine results not from declining overall food supply but from specific subgroups' declining exchange entitlements to food. While the basic shift in focus is salutary, critics such as Duffield and de Waal describe Sen as overly economistic, presenting famine victims as passive and excluding consideration of violence. They critique the food economy approach as focusing on "average" households; ignoring disparities and power relations among households; and, by aiming to quantify famine outcomes, deemphasizing analysis of dynamics and causation. De Waal stresses the importance of coping strategies as famines unfold: Choices to accept short-term hunger to avoid the long-term, irreversible sale of productive assets are crucial, and many groups begin underconsuming food early in a famine. The food economy approach, it is argued, ignores hunger as a strategic choice or food production strategies that seek not to maximize output but to minimize risks or labor use. Outsiders may thus overprioritize food needs, even in chronic situations, and not respond to local priorities of asset preservation.[21]

The food economy approach in southern Sudan is part of a larger effort by SCF—UK to improve assessments and analysis of data. A team of risk-mappers in London is attempting to quantify coping strategies in several countries. The model includes variables such as production of food and cash crops, livestock numbers and sales, lack of access to food and labor markets, and cereal prices. Political issues are dealt with to the extent to which they affect access to food.

Reducing the easily diverted items results from placing the assessment of needs in the context of overall food security. In Somalia, one donor agency is just now trying to determine local coping mechanisms. "We didn't understand this until recently," admits a donor official. "We didn't do much assistance in the livestock sector because we didn't know where the herds were or how many animals were around. There was no baseline we could use. Maybe with better information early on we could have determined the appropriate inputs. Food security is not just food."

Understanding whom agencies are responding to is also critical. "Agencies need to fully understand the sociology and ethnographic complexion of their client populations," instructs Vincent Coultan. "We still fail to differentiate by age and sex. Certainly, simple demographics need to be quantified early on and tailored to."[22]

Whom agencies talk to in assessments can also dictate inappropriate responses. In insecure areas, researchers travel by day and are often escorted by local authorities. Assessment researchers must strive to speak to representatives not only of dominant groups in each area but also of smaller, disenfranchised social groups. The gender bias is strongly tilted toward men unless it is aggressively challenged, and the escorts themselves can affect the veracity of the data, as discussed earlier. Consequently, *independence* of assessment is perhaps one of the most important policy imperatives in conflict contexts. Local groups obviously can lobby for resources, but agencies must accommodate such pressures within a strong, carefully planned framework of data collection and assessment that is as independent as possible.[23]

In southern Sudan, CRS is moving to increase accountability in the challenging context of Eastern Equatoria. CRS's program has been modified through a conscientious process of learning lessons from past experience. The agency is discussing proper methodologies for assessment with the rebel SRRA, including the modified *tukul* count, in which an empirically derived multiplier for the number of people per *tukul* is arrived at by physically counting the number of people in a predetermined pattern of *tukuls*. Camp residents are requested to stay home during the day of the *tukul* count; if movement between *tukuls* is observed, the exercise can be canceled. Acceptance of this methodology is a precondition for the continuation of the CRS program.[24]

Agencies have to be open to the data that empirical assessments produce. In Somaliland, some agencies found that the majority of civilians displaced by the resumption of conflict in 1994 were able to fend for themselves and that a major relief effort might add additional fuel to the civil war's fire. Doing nothing but active monitoring may be the most helpful response in some situations. In Goma, OFDA field staff in the camps concluded that the agency's aid was doing more harm than good, and partially based on that assessment, OFDA decided to stop its aid to those camps.

More complex assessment models do have obvious drawbacks, including a shortage of trained personnel able to carry out exercises such as participatory rural assessments (PRA). Frontline UN agency personnel—resident project officers, food monitors, sectoral experts—are often unfamiliar with PRA. Where it exists, training is usually inadequate. There is often a lack of cooperation between agricultural and animal health experts in calibrating the response to agropastoral and pastoral communities in crisis. And assessment models are often insufficiently placed in a war context, with the stresses and responses that chronic conflict produces inadequately factored in. "Training of agency personnel in assessment techniques should be a condition of [donor] funding," suggests an NGO representative.[25]

As aid programs expand to include developmentalist goals, they modify their assessment vocabulary to include "the rhetoric of participation," whereas the reality of participation is both limited and, in wartime, dangerous. Nevertheless, external agencies cannot avoid the necessity of developing the fullest knowledge (from continuous presence) of local social structures, power relations, representatives' legitimacy, and disenfranchised groups to ensure that participation in assessment does not allow the powerful to self-aggrandize.[26] Empowerment of local communities to participate in a relevant fashion is therefore critical. One donor official in Ethiopia concludes, "There is lots of pressure on local officials to inflate numbers. . . . Our objective should be to capacitate communities to be able to monitor for themselves."

With declining resources and growing impatience with diverted or misused aid, it is clear that agencies cannot (and should not) respond to all assessed "needs" beyond their capacity as outsiders. External responses will—and should—have to rely much more on local capacities to address chronic crises. "Needs assessments should be asking what a community is doing or has done, and what its current constraints are," advises a UN consultant. "When you follow that line of questioning, you find the gaps that can be filled."[27]

Commandment 3: Study Options for Modalities of Access

The various methods of negotiating and ensuring access for emergency aid can play an important role in minimizing aid's contribution to the sustenance of conflict. The access framework can be negotiated through humanitarian diplomacy; access can be achieved through cross-border operations in defiance of sovereignty claims; or it can be ensured through military or commercial means. Aid can go by road, rail, barge, air, or even donkey path. These distribution modalities are rarely examined to see whom they empower or to identify their sociological and economic ramifications. This section addresses the transportation of assistance from the point of origin to the town or village level; the transfer of commodities from that point to the end recipients will be covered in the commandment 5 section on targeting and distribution methods.

In many ways the Horn has provided groundbreaking cases in terms of crisis response. The cross-border operation into Eritrea and Ethiopia had little precedent. The corridors of tranquility agreed to in Sudan presaged a whole new approach to humanitarian action in which the UN negotiates access and NGOs implement it in the context of elaborate access agreements. And finally, the military intervention in Somalia moved the donor community closer than any previous effort to a principle of the right to food, though it crashed and burned in an attempt to rebuild a central government in which centrifugal forces were too great and Machiavellian tactics alienated key segments of the population.[28]

Negotiated Access

Negotiating access is the most common vehicle for providing assistance to populations in zones of conflict. As discussed earlier, this modality can help legitimize warring parties and provide donors with a substitute for political engagement. Access agreements are also criticized for often "reaching the lowest common denominator and [concentrating] on security of agency staff rather than of beneficiaries."[29]

The response to the long-term crisis in southern Sudan provides a model of negotiated access, the modality of choice for most agencies and donors. OLS is the first case in which warring factions have agreed over a long period of time to allow humanitarian supplies to cross lines of battle. For over half a decade, OLS has provided a channel for NGO and UN assistance to war-affected populations. As in Eritrea and Ethiopia, military intervention was not part of the response.

In Somaliland, the ICRC negotiated access through Hargeisa to affected populations in opposition-held areas. But in Ethiopia during Mengistu's rule, such negotiation was impossible until a year before the demise of his regime, and then only on a limited basis.

Major national religious bodies in Ethiopia negotiated with the government in Addis Ababa and the TPLF in Khartoum to organize a major cross-line feeding program to benefit civilians in northern Ethiopia in 1990. Although the program (Joint Relief Partnership [JRP]) was successful, both sides criticized it: The TPLF felt the program allowed too much government oversight and failed to meet agreed-upon tonnage targets; meanwhile, the government believed the insurgents' political cause was the program's main beneficiary.[30]

Negotiating access to aid people as close to their home areas as possible is an important factor in maintaining community structures critical in providing alternatives to militarized authority. Negotiating the return of displaced populations to their home areas should be a priority in all negotiated access frameworks.

In southern Sudan, switching from air to road transport entailed more benefits than the obvious one of lowering costs. Although road operations are more difficult to manage, they require more cooperation from warring parties in a way that provides some measure of conditionality.[31]

The humanitarian diplomacy that produces negotiated access agreements holds the promise of much wider benefits beyond aid movement. As a DHA concept paper urges, "Humanitarian diplomacy should aim at broadening the scope of incentives to promote peace, cooperation, and reconciliation."[32]

Military Force

Military force has been used in several ways: to guard refugee camps, to protect relief convoys and assets, and to actually distribute relief supplies. While many praise increasing military involvement in humanitarian relief as a positive, rights-protective step, others fear a new era of relief assistance as political crisis management. The tremendous costs divert resources from nonemergency development aid and conflict resolution initiatives as well as creating perceptions that geopolitics rather than human need will increasingly drive aid decisions as they merge with foreign policy. This perception can lead to combatants targeting aid workers more often.

Moreover, military humanitarianism when not accompanied by political engagement positions aid as merely a technical fix rather than a search for long-term solutions. This situation can help to legitimate military protagonists (via negotiated access) and fuel the war economy. Moreover, military protection itself can be corrupted and move from protecting to violating human rights.[33] Other problematic issues include duplication of services and differences in standards and cultures between military and humanitarian responders, the impossibility of sustaining military protection, the lack of responsiveness of military structures to civilian complaints and needs, and the nontransparency of military responses.

Military humanitarianism—though hopelessly late and arguably inappropriate at the time it was employed—was a large part of the response to the crisis in Somalia. Operation Restore Hope represents the first case in which UN forces were committed without the consent of a standing government, which did not exist in Somalia at the time of the intervention in December 1992. The limited humanitarian mandate at the outset of the intervention was eclipsed by broader policy goals and political decisions that went far beyond the original intent of the operation.[34]

The obsession with security and protecting commodities drove the response at the end of 1992, rather than the search for strategies that would avoid direct distributions by agencies that were vulnerable to diversion and extortion.

A study conducted by the Refugee Policy Group concludes that the military intervention between December 1992 and May 1993 saved between 10,000 and 25,000 lives, far fewer than figures constantly cited by U.S. and UN policymakers and spokespersons. "Four billion dollars could have gone a long way to strengthening the self-reliance and future resilience of local communities," observes one food security expert. "The women and the weather helped more than the troops."[35]

The United Nations Assistance Mission in Rwanda (UNAMIR) was deployed in Rwanda well before the genocide began. Despite the political decision to withdraw most of the soldiers under UNAMIR and gut its mandate, the peacekeepers were able to directly save lives by protecting up to 20,000 people in Kigali with small arms and barbed wire. The safe havens the international forces provided should be analyzed fully for their potential future role in protecting civilians from slaughter.

The French Operation Turquoise, designed to facilitate humanitarian aid in the southwest corner of Rwanda, performed well on technical grounds but created major political problems in two areas. First, it provided a safe haven for retreating government officials, military officers, and militia members, allowing and even aiding their orderly exodus into Zaire. Second, it undermined the UN's efforts to get troop commitments for UNAMIR and weakened multilateral intervention objectives. On the other hand, the operation protected roughly 14,000 at-risk civilians inside Rwanda and helped improve security and massively increase humanitarian aid in mid-1994.

When military contingents—including those of the United States—were sent to Goma, they responded directly to emergency needs but did not have a mandate to address the insecurity in the camps. Logistical costs for foreign military contingents were considerably higher than for commercial suppliers. The multidonor evaluation of the Rwandan response concludes that the comparative advantage enjoyed by the military is usually short-lived and applicable only in special circumstances. Specific questions arise as to the military's predictability, effectiveness, cost, and cooperative abilities.[36]

In an unprecedented move that signaled the desperation of organizing officials, two battalions of Zairian troops were hired to maintain security in the Rwandan camps in Zaire. The UN secretary general failed to obtain an international police force for Rwandan refugee camps in Zaire. The UNHCR therefore paid the Zairian government to deploy soldiers under joint Zairian and international control to maintain law and order, prevent intimidation of and escort returnees, and guarantee UN and NGO security. An international civilian liaison group helps monitor Zairian troops deployed in Rwandan refugee camps; mediates between the Zairian force, the UNHCR and NGOs, and refugee leaders; and investigates security breaches and soldiers' abuses or indiscipline. (Tanzanian police— paid by the government and supported by UNHCR—patrolled the Tanzanian camps and partially addressed the question of impunity by arresting some of the troublemakers.)

The Zairian force has partially succeeded in its limited role but has no mandate to arrest suspected genocide participants, stop arms flows and militarization, or halt militia border incursions from Rwanda.[37] "It worked out far beyond expectations," says one veteran official. "The troops had a major positive effect on the camps; law and order have improved." Fairly unorthodox methods were employed to achieve a semblance of that law and order: People who led demonstrations were arrested and often jailed and beaten by the soldiers. "This has lessened the authority of some of the leaders in the eyes of the people," claims one official, and the immediate issue of impunity for criminal actions in the camps was partially addressed.

A contrary position is supported by other observers. This less sanguine view points out that the Zairian troops have not dealt with separating the bulk of the civilian population from the militia, nor have they arrested those accused of crimes against humanity. The soldiers of the former government still had their own camps and were receiving arms, all the while strengthening their capacity to launch cross-border incursions into Rwanda. Other questionable by-products of the use of the Zairian forces have resulted, including the resuscitation of the Mobutu regime, a third party that is not neutral to the conflict in Rwanda. Furthermore, Kathi Austin found that the Zairian forces were complicit in the military agendas of the former Rwandan political and military leadership and that they engaged in serious looting, extortion, and a variety of human rights abuses. She reports one incident in which a member of the Zairian security force was shot by a Rwandan refugee. In retaliation, Zairian security forces lobbed a mortar shell into an NGO compound and shot at refugees in the camp near an orphanage, killing thirty-seven refugees, most of whom were women and children.[38]

Similar obstruction and manipulation are practiced by leaders of refugee camps in Kenya. In Kakuma camp in 1993, camp leaders organized a boycott of the census. The leaders of the boycott were arrested by Kenyan authorities at the urging of agency officials. Without knowing the power structure of the camps, this action would have been impossible. Knowing the power structure also often leads to understanding the rackets of diversion and corruption usually embedded in long-term aid recipient communities.

In eastern Ethiopia, lootings escalated during July 1995, affecting UN agencies, NGOs, and indigenous organizations. Historically, the populations through which commodities from Djibouti passed on their way to Dire Dawa were given a "tax" in sugar to allow safe passage. Since the upsurge in lootings, the government has decided to provide armed escorts for convoys, another available military option in the protection of aid.

Private security forces are also being utilized. Executive Outcomes and Defense Service Limited are two companies that have been hired to protect humanitarian supplies.

Commercial Channels

The search for more secure and less militarized channels to bring commodities into Somalia has led agencies to utilize commercial channels. WFP has sold commodities to Somali merchants in Mombasa, then contracted with the merchants to transport the goods to targeted sites, where WFP buys the commodities back. A variation on this theme of commercializing aid deliveries is to directly contract with merchants (or private cooperatives) to buy commodities and transport them to their distribution destination, allowing the merchants roughly a 10 percent profit margin, payable upon receipt of goods at the destination. "Instead of 60 percent being ripped off, we could have 10 percent markups," asserts a European donor official. "Merchants have all their own arrangements," says David Neff, country director of CARE—Somalia. "The salient point is that the commodities belong to individuals."[39] A prominent Somali merchant agrees: "If WFP comes, the militias will loot. If the bags say 'Gift of the USA,' they will be looted. But if the goods are in the possession of businessmen, they will be safe. Businessmen will pay for security and make deals to move."

The security of the goods is ensured principally by the deterrence afforded by the certainty of clan retribution. For example, when a Habr Gedir militia looted a Rahanweyne (Leyson) businessman in Mogadishu in June 1995, the Leyson captured five Habr Gedir trucks and held them until compensation was given. "The days of agencies controlling distributions are over," says Ali Salad Hassan of UNDP—Somalia.[40] Willet Weeks agrees: "Greater reliance on market-based solutions and commercial channels will be more effective than messy direct distributions."[41]

Of course, no method is a panacea. Although this commercial approach reduces the number of armed men employed by agencies for security as well as reducing diversion, it can empower merchants who are the financiers of particular warlords. Agencies must be very careful to understand and avoid cartels that try to manipulate markets and bring malnutrition levels up in order to increase the international response, and hence their profits. In some contexts, agencies will have to choose their poison.

Monetization is also used as a method of getting a diversified set of commodities into the market as well as raising local currency for small-scale rehabilitation projects. However, monetization is an inappropriate response when the purchasing power of affected populations has collapsed. Monetization also requires in-depth understanding of the commercial networks in a society and a reasonable analysis of how monetized commodities will affect markets.

The limits of monetization in terms of inadequate purchasing power are seen in mid-1995 studies conducted by AICF in Bay Region in Somalia. The studies found that the global malnutrition rate for children six to twenty-nine months of age was 25.7 percent, and only 16 percent of families had access to food on the market. The study concluded, "In view of the good sorghum harvests in the last two seasons, . . . the precarious nutritional situation in the area could be partly due to the lack of variation in diets, caused by the population's lack of income and their inability to purchase other foodstuffs and sources of nutrition on the markets."[42]

(Outside the Greater Horn, in the town of Dubrovnik in the former Yugoslavia, UNICEF—backed by the European Union [EU] and the Italian government—decided to go through a Serb blockade to bring in medicine and evacuate women and children. In each convoy, half of the goods transported were relief and half were commercial items arranged by local traders. Money was made in addition to the unmolested movement of relief supplies. The Serbs eventually lifted the blockade.)

Donors have bandied about numerous ideas about moving commodities since UNOSOM's departure. "We've suggested using shopkeepers, mosques," offers a donor official. "But these ideas are laughed at by most people. Instead, most everyone is looking at the old way of getting assurances from Aidid."

In northern Ethiopia, agencies provided resources for the local purchase of commodities for redistribution in deficit areas. Local purchase promotes food production and market integration and reduces overall costs. But major purchases can accelerate inflationary pressures in local markets. It is critical that local purchase schemes not price local consumers and traders out of the market, which undermines access to food and the development of commercial markets.[43]

Non-negotiated Access

Cross-border access options often defy a sovereign government's prohibitions against accessing vulnerable populations in war-torn areas. For aid agencies, "cross-border operations tend to reflect not only the political and military divisions within the country," points out Stein Villumstad, "but tend also to divide the aid community. Information is in danger of being fragmented and incompatible."[44]

The diversification of entry points for emergency supplies—especially employing cross-border initiatives—is a strategy that can reduce the unintended empowering of a particular authority. Utilizing various cross-border channels or smaller ports (or even beach landings, as in the case of the ICRC in Somalia in 1992) can lessen the dependence agencies have on particular large-scale extortion networks but may create smaller ones. In addition, diversification may not be feasible logistically, topographically, or economically.

In Sudan, where the government periodically threatens to close down the southern sector of OLS and force commodities to go through government channels, contingency plans are debated by agencies that would refuse to succumb to that kind of control. An expansion of cross-border channels from Ethiopia, Uganda, Kenya, Zaire, and the Central African Republic would likely be the only alternative. The rationale for increased risk (Ugandan rebels) and cost (Zairian extortion) is to avoid further empowering the Sudanese government through all of the fringe benefits it accrues as outlined earlier.

Support for the cross-border operation into Eritrea and northern Ethiopia in the mid-1980s represented an early example of humanitarian intervention. Both the EPLF and TPLF, the two principal movements fighting the central government in Addis Ababa until their victories in 1991, developed the political practice of linking mass mobilization with the provision of public welfare. The humanitarian wings of the political movements, the Eritrean Relief Association (ERA) and the Relief Society of Tigray (REST), were the conduits through which external aid passed, aid that primarily came from the Emergency Relief Desk (ERD) consortium. These indigenous local organizations provide a model of efficiency, accountability, and local capacity building for other complex political emergencies.[45]

Regional Responses, Legal
Questions, and Enforcement Mechanisms

In situations of regional instability and interrelated conflict across borders, the response should obviously be framed as regionally as possible. Staff from the same agencies can have totally different perceptions of common problems across borders. Quite often, the available principles and conventions are not applicable to these complex regional emergencies.

For example, the status of refugees and internally displaced persons is a false dichotomy, especially in regions where borders divide identity groups. Although normally these two categories of displaced people are treated differently in terms of assistance and protection (primarily because of the distinction created by UNHCR's mandate), on the border of Somaliland and Region Five (the Somali Region of Ethiopia, popularly known as the Ogaden) some agencies have refused to engage in a conventional refugee program for populations that moved from Somaliland to Region Five. "We looked at this population as if they were displaced on both sides of the border, so as to not draw people artificially out of their home country," says a UN consultant.[46]

The Greater Horn of Africa Initiative (spearheaded by the U.S. government) formulates a regional framework as its starting point.

But agencies usually don't cross borders with ease. Vincent Coultan explains further:

> If we accept that public welfare provision is already irreversibly internationalized, driven by massive Northern charitable actions these past years, then donors and agencies should take more responsibility for offering "seamless accompaniment" of refugees as they move home.
>
> Emergency life-sustaining interventions are best linked to strategies that reliably enhance communities' resilience to the stresses of their future environment. Refugee populations, especially at the point of their repatriation, are often abandoned to that vulnerability, since aid monies, convention has it, can be redirected upon reaching that symbolic turning point (and are). Sustained support providing upliftment of the livelihoods of returnees once home is in no way guaranteed. Many agencies, while calling themselves international, are somewhat border-blinkered in outlook, view their programs from solely a national-internal perspective, do not talk that regularly to their neighboring country offices, and are often ill informed as to the earlier activities and achievements of their colleagues over the border.
>
> Inevitably there are examples of returnee populations who all too soon face stresses that outstrip their capacities, once more becoming displaced or otherwise in great need. The short-sightedness, evidenced in not accompanying communities and promoting their rehabilitation that critical step further, ultimately costs the international community dearly. Families that simply do not have the opportunity to rebuild the diversity of their traditional asset base once home are often knocked down by erstwhile surmountable cyclical crises, gaining undeserved reputations of helplessness. New subregional perspectives on rational resilience-bolstering strategies are timely. Certainly, the institutional barriers of agencies' own making will have to be eroded. By adopting rational strategies, all stakeholders will be rewarded in the longer term with higher returns on their humanitarian investments.[47]

The root causes and solutions to the problems of refugees and internally displaced persons are often the same. In 1992, UNHCR and a handful of NGOs operating in the Somali refugee camps in northeast Kenya went rapidly to a cross-border operation to contain refugee flows and prevent refugee camps from becoming lighthouses for affected populations in both countries. Minimizing dislocation should be a primary objective of access frameworks. As discussed earlier, displaced populations are more easily manipulated by warleaders, and subsistence economies that more directly support traditional and civilian leadership are undermined by dislocation.

Also noted earlier are the myriad examples of aid operations helping to sustain conflict by their locations. In the Rwandan camps in Zaire, the wild panic that such operations were in during the first couple of months after the genocide was not useful in relocating recipient sites. Nevertheless, "soon after we could have moved aid back farther away from the border," says a UN official. "But wrong political analysis led people to think that the refugees would return very soon."

There are international legal questions surrounding situations like the pursuit of Aidid and the presence of genocide perpetrators in the Rwandan camps. Arrest orders are complicated by the lack of an enforcement body to implement international conventions or decisions. Humanitarian organizations—along with civilians in the impacted area—are often the principal victims of such erratic enforcement and are even blamed (only sometimes justifiably) for not dealing with the ties between civilian populations and war criminals, at times solidified by situations in which populations are concentrated for distribution of relief supplies.

To separate the genocide organizers from the civilian populations in Goma, for example, would have required extremely specialized military forces that would have had to isolate hundreds of people in a sea of hundreds of thousands of people who inevitably would have been terrorized into providing shelter and protection to the leaders. "It would have catalyzed a confrontation," says Rowland Roome of CARE—Rwanda. "The analysis was correct all along, but the means to address the problem were too difficult."[48] The fruitless, violent hunt for Aidid in Somalia undoubtedly played into the decision not to send a UN force to Rwanda to counter the genocide. In November 1994, NGOs and UN camp managers publicly called for international peacekeeping forces to separate civilian populations from warleaders. After months of inaction, the Zairian troops were finally deployed, a halfway measure that addressed the worst symptoms but left the root causes untouched.

Commandment 4: Be Astute and
Flexible in the Types of Aid Provided

The selection of the kind of assistance that is employed plays a major role in the extent to which that aid sustains conflict. This choice is critical for three particular reasons. First, certain kinds of inputs are more easily looted or more valuable than others and draw the attention of unsavory elements more quickly. Second, some aid strategies simply respond to symptoms and can promote dependency, whereas other aid can promote subsistence and thus undergird traditional community structures and efforts to protect livelihoods. Third, in some cases targeting assistance directly to military authorities in order to reduce their predatory behavior toward local populations makes sense.

Emergencies that require interventions in the Greater Horn (and elsewhere) are consistently misinterpreted as food emergencies. But food shortfalls or inaccessibility are usually only a symptom of deeper, structural problems that food aid sometimes can even exacerbate. Better assessment and analysis can lead to a more appropriate mix of inputs and policy responses that would include much less food than do most current interventions.

Flexibility is a key concept in providing agencies with the tools to reduce their contribution to conflict. Although there are significant logistical and political obstacles, donor mandates should be more flexible to allow local-appropriate responses unfettered by overrated distinctions between relief and development. (Although donors have become more aware of the importance of prevention, resources are still harder to obtain for prevention than for cure.) Agencies must be flexible to respond to fast-changing conflict contexts.

Sustainability should also be a guiding principle. National social welfare systems underwritten by large foreign aid programs are a thing of the past in many countries affected by chronic conflict. Linear development models completely fail to capture current realities. Tax bases are grossly inadequate, and development aid budgets are shrinking globally. Attempts to reproduce Western-style state-administered welfare programs are unsustainable. Much more rethinking must be done regarding appropriate basic-needs responses. External response to these emergencies should be driven by what already works at the local level, what structures are already in place and supported by the community, what the indigenous social welfare mechanisms and kinship exchange dynamics are in a society, and so on. "We must take our cue from the successes on the ground," asserts Matthew Bryden of the UN Emergency Unit. Filling the holes in the social safety net is critical, but "for the rest, we should be working with the private sector and supporting their initiatives."[49]

Lootable Versus Nonlootable Aid

Types of aid that less easily feed conflict are situation-specific, but in general a food's market value can play a major role in whether it draws the interest of military forces and looters. The ease of converting direct food aid to cash makes it easier for militaries to exploit than agricultural rehabilitation programs.[50] Internationally donated rice in

Somalia reached legendary status in terms of its attractiveness to looters, whereas sorghum drew little interest. "Somalia starkly illustrates the perils of relying on high-value commodities," affirms an aid official.[51] CARE reported an experience in the Juba Valley in which one of its convoys was attacked by looters, but upon discovering that the contents were sorghum, the looters departed, leaving the trucks and their contents untouched. The strategy of OFDA and some other agencies by mid-1992 was to flood the country with maize, bulgur wheat, and sorghum instead of rice.[52]

ICRC moved to cooked food in hundreds of kitchens in Somalia to reduce the interest of looters. In many cases, blended foods—nutritionally high in value but less appealing to the taste—could be considered because they are appropriate as general rations rather than only as emergency food for severely malnourished children. Blended foods—powdered, vitamin-fortified blends of cereals, pulses, and possibly milk and sugar—are not too expensive for such use, and there is less likelihood of their diversion for adult consumption.[53] Foods that can be stored for extended periods of time for communities that keep their supplies buried in grain stores to avoid preying militias should also be considered. Southern Sudanese have expanded cassava production because it has proven useful in crises, as in Mozambique and Liberia: It resists insects and can be left in the ground for three years as a food reserve safe from looters.[54]

(But in the context of searching for lower-value interventions, Geoffry Loane reminds aid providers: "We never should underestimate the damage done to the dignity of those receiving aid. They have few rights and poor self-esteem; they are degraded, marginalized, and usually cannot fulfill their social and family obligations."[55])

When providing seeds, part of the equation for selection of particular varieties should include their value to looters, their storage capacity, their time of germination (fast-yielding varieties in situations of chronic insecurity are often favored), and their quality (better, more adaptable seed is mobile in the sense that displaced populations take it with them). Seed programs can create problems if they begin to dilute the rich heterogeneity that allows communities to survive. "In Rwanda, there are 300 types of bean seed," says a food security adviser. "Aid agencies in a rush can make the situation worse."[56]

One of the biggest killers in complex emergencies is measles. In many conflict areas, there are extremely low rates of immunization. Expanded programs of immunizations (EPIs), or at least measles vaccinations, should be undertaken as widely and early on in a war zone as possible. To wit, Refugee Policy Group's study of the emergency response in Somalia found that preventive public health and primary care measures could have prevented the deaths of over 150,000 people in 1992.[57]

Another input relatively unattractive to war participants is educational materials. UNICEF and some NGOs are trying to get educational services up and running as early as possible. UNICEF's "school in a box" programs attempt to get teachers back to teaching and materials in the hands of students in situations of instability. "The program aims to put normality back into disaster situations," says a UNICEF official. "It can be introduced immediately in an emergency, anywhere."[58] Education has traditionally not been considered part of an emergency response package. In the late 1980s in Angola and Afghanistan, for example, there was no educational component in UNICEF's programming. But even educational inputs must be carefully thought through, as Kathi Austin illustrates: "Educational services that are usually given in the local language can become tools by which authorities can propagandize the youth. In the eastern Zaire camps, schoolchildren in some locations were taught war chants and would sing incitements to kill Tutsi in front of relief workers who did not know the language and praised the children's performances."[59]

Promoting Subsistence and Protecting Livelihoods

Responding to all assessed needs is impossible, as needs in many war-torn societies are theoretically infinite. A crucial alternative framework for response is that of protecting livelihoods and preventing further degeneration of a community's capacity to adapt to chronic crisis and manage its own response to these crisis cycles. "Any means that can be provided to be self-supporting should be utilized," asserts Geoffry Loane. "This allows people to assume roles and responsibilities, to have dignity. Aid must be targeted to the globality of the human problem."[60]

Providing rehabilitative inputs to women's groups and women heads of households—especially in the context of complex emergencies, when women shoulder an even greater burden in terms of household food security because of the absence of men—is perhaps the most critical strategy undergirding community adaptation to crisis and supporting survival mechanisms. Even in an emergency context, income-generation projects can provide purchasing power for families who cannot access their entire food needs through their own production or through the market.

Some analysts have argued that food aid should be avoided as much as possible. For example, the Sobat River in southern Sudan and the Juba River in Somalia have at times teemed with fish while trucks and planes roared in with food that was diverted in large quantities. Some agencies have provided hooks, nets, and twine, and creative offshoots such as bush shops and fishing export businesses have resulted, but food aid has been the predominant response in terms of overall resources.

Beyond subsistence, there is tremendous potential for wealth creation as well. Commercial fishing, agricultural diversification, and livestock exports all provide attractive livelihoods, particularly for current or potential members of militias or armed forces.

Another rationale for increasing the ratio of nonfood to food inputs is the minimal military ramifications inherent in most nonfood rehabilitative aid. One donor agency claims to be getting out of food aid altogether. "The military is not interested in our rehabilitative inputs. This way we are reempowering local structures."

OLS has evolved significantly from a near complete devotion to humanitarian services (primarily free food distribution) to wider development goals, including food security and capacity building. The consortium has increasingly emphasized inputs for food production (fishing, agriculture, and livestock), which local people need and warring parties are less likely to divert.

As part of a broader strategy of subsistence restoration, some agencies operating in Western Equatoria in southern Sudan are encouraging surplus food production to help restore some of the commercial networks that existed before the war. World Vision has bought food from Yambio District and moved it to Tonj, reducing externally provided food aid. On the broader regional level, some agencies are increasingly supporting regional markets by buying surplus from one country and sending or trading the commodities to another, e.g., buying in Uganda for southern Sudan and Rwanda.

Another view is forwarded by Vincent Coultan: "Agencies are often too lazy to build developmental objectives into their emergency programs. Here, the donor community carries a responsibility along with significant power of leverage to insist that agencies imbue these principles earlier on."[61] But some agencies are moving toward making the incorporation of developmental objectives into relief a standard practice. For example, in a long-term emergency like Sudan, there are low-cost but high-impact interventions that can greatly reduce vulnerability and that many agencies are carrying out. These are classic development-in-relief, portable interventions such as fishing nets and vaccinations.

More generally, though, "there is such a dearth of resources for rehabilitation and so much for relief; it's feast and famine," says a donor official. "We should be able to hold on to some of the avalanche of emergency funding and to consciously do rehabilitation." But an extremely important dilemma obstructs flexibility, that is, as one analyst points out, "The most widely available commodity in relief crises is food from donor stocks. Other items require cash."

Commandment 5: Study Impacts of Targeting and Distribution Methods

The commandment 3 section on access modalities covered movement of commodities to affected areas; this section looks at methodologies of getting assistance directly into the hands of affected populations. Again, decisions about how and to whom aid is targeted can have important ramifications for the balance of authority at the local level. Some key principles are operative here: promoting gender sensitivity, demanding independent management, supporting alternative structures and moderate voices. Also, agencies must improve targeting by making registration, distribution, and monitoring more transparent and by informing local people of their rights.[62]

It is imperative for agencies to understand patterns of political and social marginalization in order to develop distribution structures for their assistance that target those most seriously affected by conflict. There is usually great differentiation in suffering within a community along class and identity lines. Navigating along these fault lines is a critical ingredient in the recipe for minimizing the offtake from aid to warring parties. It is necessary that agencies understand the internal social relations within a community that often predetermine who will receive how much aid in any given distribution. One donor official suggests, "Agencies should not have to understand and analyze these issues by themselves. There should be a way to do this collectively and save resources as well as to generate new analysis and consensus when possible."

In a review of decades of experience in distributing commodities, Oxfam—UK/Ireland concluded that the accuracy of registration largely determines whether a distribution will successfully get inputs into the hands of affected families. The registration should document the numbers and location of the affected populations, the social profile of the affected community, the unit of distribution, and the criteria of eligibility. "The more open and simple the distribution system is," the study concludes, "the more people will understand it and their role within it. Understanding builds trust and confidence both in the system and between people."[63]

As the 1980s progressed, donors increasingly used NGOs to

deliver commodities to famine-affected populations in government-
held areas of Ethiopia, bypassing the host government as much as
possible. This approach is in contrast to the distribution structures in
the rebel-held areas of Ethiopia and Eritrea, where local agencies
planned, managed, and transported everything.

ICRC institutionally maintained independent control of distribution structures in government-held areas of Ethiopia during the war.
"It was a textbook operation for ICRC," says a Red Cross veteran.
"We had independent supervision and beneficiaries from both sides
of the conflict." More broadly, "independent monitoring and management of aid is critical to avoid charges of partiality. Aid should be
individualized and witnessed as much as possible. Witness is the key
to successful distributions."[64]

In Somalia, says a donor official, this external control was delu-
sional. "Aid gets distributed though locals anyway, whether it's the
local staff of international agencies or the elders. The international
staff provides a political buffer; they give an out to local staff to blame
outsiders for maintaining certain standards and objectives."

Getting aid directly into the hands of families—especially
women heads of households—is an important objective in eroding
the power of military authorities. For example, in the Rwandan
refugee camps, "we started out by dumping aid at the prefecture
level," related a UN official in mid-1995. "We then moved to the com-
mune, and then the cell. Now we are going to individual families.
When the distribution mechanism is not at the family level, there is a
problem." In the Rwandan refugee camps, distributing goods at
higher levels of social organization than the family perpetuates the
authority of the military and political structure that planned and executed the genocide. It must be noted, though, that the speed with
which people crossed the border into Tanzania and Zaire from
Rwanda made it imperative to work with whatever structure could
be identified in the immediacy of the crisis. "It was only possible to
do mass distributions because of the existing structure," explains one
agency official. "Using existing structures is usually good."

The multidonor evaluation of the Rwandan emergency response
also concluded that direct distributions to women is an important
option to consider. Furthermore, the study made the following rec-
ommendation to operational agencies:

> Develop and get inter-agency and, to the extent feasible, from the
> relevant governmental authorities, advance agreement on opera-
> tional guidelines for food distribution. These guidelines should pro-
> vide for direct distribution of food at household level if there is a

risk of exploitation of the food distribution system by camp leadership. They should also recommend exploring the desirability and feasibility of direct provision to women.[65]

As well as overinflated population figures, a major cause of diversion is flawed distribution systems. Family ration cards should be put into place as quickly as possible, and the exercise should be repeated as often as possible.

Where it is feasible politically and culturally, women should be the actual recipients of inputs and heavily involved in the planning process. "We can't leave planning in the hands of technocratic food distributors," says Willet Weeks.[66] Women for the most part are the custodians of the family's welfare and the pillars of the social structure and usually know best who the most vulnerable families in a community are. "There are different traditional structures," observes one agency veteran. "Women are more related to the original structures than the visible authorities. Women also traditionally are more egalitarian than men." But elevating women too much can expose them to retribution in some places, so agencies must be sensitive to the limits of externally driven social engineering.

Women should be leaders in distributions in refugee camps as well. Roberta Cohen gives two examples outside the Greater Horn: "In camps along the Thai-Cambodian border, the provision of rations to women and girls reduced the diversion of food to the military. In Malawi, when women became involved in distribution, complaints from refugee women about being forced to give sexual favors or money in exchange for food largely ended." She also points out that UNHCR's own Guidelines on the Protection of Refugee Women suggest that refugee women should control distribution structures to the maximum extent possible.[67]

Some strategies explicitly attempt to build up alternative structures so as to have input alongside or to challenge existing military ones. In the Bahr al-Ghazal region of southern Sudan, WFP has established Relief Committees, popularly elected bodies intended to be involved in the planning and logistics of distribution to the community. The Relief Committees arose from recognition of the diminished authority and effectiveness of chiefs and the difficulty inherent in micromanaging all distributions. The Relief Committees were inspired by Oxfam's Northern Kenyan food aid operation, in which community-based relief committees facilitate both distribution and feedback from recipients about their changing food security.[68]

Again, a major rationale for this kind of strategy is that the most important insurance policy against diversion and other abuses of humanitarian intent is the encouragement of community empowerment and local groups holding authorities accountable. "The Relief Committees will publicly announce what is being delivered to the community," says one donor official. "This enhances local accountability. It is harder for the SRRA to rip the people off." The committees are also intended to improve and widen participation in decisionmaking about the needs of a community, especially promoting women in the process in their role as primary food providers to the household and community.

Seven women and six men comprise each committee. The women select the vulnerable families who will be recipients of a distribution. WFP plans to involve women more in the monitoring in the future. Current responsibilities of a Relief Committee include acting as information sources on the local food economy; as a focal point for communication; and as partners in the distribution process in targeting, developing distribution strategies, managing logistics, screening, and evaluating for future planning.[69]

A major problem with the WFP Relief Committees is that in their hasty creation there was very little coordination between the Relief Committees and existing structures, whether indigenous to the community, part of the SPLA's fledgling local government, or external constructs such as the church-organized Joint Relief Committees. The extent to which these committees will undermine traditional authority structures or truly enable community involvement is not yet determined. "Traditional values have their elements of repression, but there was a certain cohesiveness to the community," avers a UN official. "We can't go back to the past, but we must find a way to assist communities rediscover those indigenous values."[70] There are other constraints and failures in donor efforts to train and support effective grassroots local relief committees: limited staff time, dispersed communities difficult to gather quickly for meetings, lack of regular meetings of all involved, lack of field-level training for Relief Association of Southern Sudan (RASS) and SRRA representatives, and WFP and OLS workers' "failure to realize it is their duty to invest the time, patience, and openness to train and support the relief committee members."[71] There is also the fundamental question about the sustainability of externally created entities at the local level that will only be answered by the degree to which local communities take genuine ownership of the concept.

African Rights questions the degree to which participation is genuine in a relief context:

It has to be recognized that the kind of community "participation" induced when one provides relief supplies is very superficial. To go beyond this, an aid agency needs a thorough understanding of the society in which it works, and a sustained dialogue with the people. A few agencies, such as Adventist Development and Relief Association (ADRA) and Africa Action in Need (AAIN), are trying to follow this road, at least to the extent of employing local community development staff, and meeting repeatedly with leaders of the population.[72]

Agencies in the Sudan Emergency Operations Consortium (SEOC) that are facing targeting dilemmas in Sudan have more aggressively begun to hand aid to local relief committees. This action is based on the committees' agreement to target the most vulnerable, widely publicize distribution, and personally participate in and take responsibility for reporting on distributions.[73]

A Sudanese employee of one NGO in Sudan held a series of chiefs' meetings to address the lack of accountability and independence with which the traditional structures were burdened. "There were no legal recourses for the imbalances of power being exploited," observes this field officer. The discussions focused on the phenomenon of victimization and predation and on the community's vision of the future. "People don't know that they too have the capacity to bring about peace." One executive chief from the area confirms the process, saying that this NGO "involves the executive chiefs, the sub-chiefs, and the *gol* leaders in the distribution process. The civil administration and the district commissioner decide the tax, and the SRRA has nothing to decide."

From the government-held area of southern Sudan comes an example of agency collaboration that minimized the involvement of military authorities. A number of agencies operating in Juba established Combined Agency Relief Team (CART) to increase the involvement of local communities in decisionmaking about and distribution of aid.

In the Rwandan camps, agencies' promotion of alternative representation takes the form of encouraging women's groups and technical committees (water, health, etc.) in order to bypass the military structures. Agencies have traversed more dangerous ground in attempting to elect or recruit new management structures for the delivery of food aid, the form of aid most coveted of course by the former government structure in keeping its authority intact. In Goma, for example, CARE facilitated the creation of groups of young men—"scouts"—who were entrusted with organizing distribution mechanisms. The scout group had a falling out with the *interahamwe*

(Hutu militia) leadership, and the heads of both the local *interahamwe* group and the scout group were executed. CARE had to evacuate its staff, and all of the other scouts were murdered. The scouts had been cultivated as an alternative structure but were seen as a potential threat to the militias.

There are religious communities in the Juba Valley of Somalia that primarily cater to Bantu populations, such as those in Beled Karim and Mana Mofa. These communities could provide legitimate vehicles for distribution to Bantu communities, which will likely experience chronic food insecurity due to the broader instability of the region.

One overarching strategy in the development of alternative leadership in some instances could be to attempt to achieve a collective strategy among all agencies of refusing to deal with rights-abusing military leaders. This would be a daunting political and logistical task with important fiscal implications. It is likely that only in extreme cases would this type of strategy be undertaken.

Taxation of relief inputs is a given in most war situations. What some of the aforementioned initiatives do is create additional accountability and reciprocity between community and authority. When access and distribution modalities ensure that aid gets into the hands of the intended targets, they reduce the major diversions of aid that reinforce the unaccountable military culture, and they force the authority to approach the local communities and request or demand a certain share. Then distribution becomes a matter of negotiation between authority and community. Some authorities are obviously more abusive than others and will take what they want. But this approach of course has deleterious impacts on the support they receive from their "constituents" in the long term.

Commandment 6: Standardize Costs and Minimize Extortion and Hyperinflation

In studying the extent to which aid feeds conflict, analysts often tend to focus on the diversion of inputs and other visible signs of sustenance and overlook the other economic by-products of agency operations and how they might reinforce military authorities or war economies. Controlling these costs—especially physical costs—is a critical element of an overall strategy to reduce aid's contribution to conflict.

It is extremely difficult to impose standards on a group of agencies with their own parochial mandates and cost structures. "Each organization has its own needs," acknowledges an agency official. "No decision can be binding. Nevertheless, consultative processes and aspirations toward standardization are important. Imposed solutions don't work, but consultation does."[74]

In attempting to negotiate on behalf of agency consortiums, there must be unanimity among all agencies. For example, all agencies operating in Baidoa collaborated to cut vehicle costs. Before Aidid's invasion in September 1995, further efforts were being made in that town to standardize payments among all UN agencies and NGOs. Also in Somalia, UN agencies developed the UN Common Wage Policy in mid-1995, which standardizes the payments to certain categories of national personnel such as security guards, storekeepers, and other local support staff. In Rwanda, SCF—UK was helpful from the outset in organizing some NGOs inside the country on housing, transport, and local salaries. In Goma, UNHCR and the NGOs got together and put ceilings on what they would pay for labor costs, resulting in a 50 percent reduction in salaries in one day.

As newcomers enter an area, it is important that they consult with agencies already operating there. In eastern Ethiopia, "we canvassed all of the other agencies and found average costs for different services before we started," says an agency official.

Unequal currency exchange is another area that can help underwrite military activities. In government-held areas of Sudan, agencies and donors successfully put strong pressure on the Sudanese government to end its dual exchange-rate system, which was extremely unfair to agencies. In Somalia, major agencies such as UNDP have increased the number of currency dealers whom they use, making the bids more competitive and attempting to "spread the wealth" over different subclans.

Any cost-containment strategy must address the extraordinary overheads that plague most emergency operations, especially UN agencies. Accountability on overhead is totally lacking. There is little standardization of equipment purchasing to reduce costs. UN expatriate salaries are sometimes shockingly out of line with the salaries of international and local NGOs. More credibility for the quest to reduce extortion-based costs would exist if internal houses were put in order.

Commandment 7: Commit to
Independent Monitoring and Evaluation

A commitment to adequate, independent monitoring and a willingness to continuously evaluate programs are key elements in reducing aid's contribution to conflict. Once funded, programs often don't undergo prompt review.

SEOC's evaluation notes that the consortium has inadequately supervised the distribution—and failed to monitor the end use—of food aid in nongovernment areas, which has often been a magnet for disorganized populations. It notes that military and other diversions have left only nutritionally irrelevant amounts of food, transported at high cost, for the many hungry civilians. Field reports that are "based upon hopes and assumptions rather than actuality" and minimize political problems exacerbate a lack of data—beyond tonnages divided by assumed population numbers—to substantiate claims for beneficiaries.[75]

There are far too few resources spent on quality monitoring. Conscientious logistical plans that attempt to reduce diversion and other negative externalities require more monitors, which require more resources. Nonetheless, more experienced, better-trained monitors are required in complex emergency situations.

One agency delivering large amounts of food to Rwanda increased its monitoring rapidly just after the emergency erupted in 1994. "We went from 120 tons per month diversion to five tons per month within Rwanda between July 1993 and January 1994," recalls a representative of that international agency. "We did it through monitoring. It's monotonous, boring, but critical in cutting down mismanagement." In Angola, increasing the monitors through field sub-offices throughout the country reduced diversion as well.

Monitoring can be intimidating because it can uncover major problems and faults with responding agencies. "In Sudan in 1988 and Somalia in 1991, agencies weren't confident to respond, not only because of the insecurity and difficulty of access but also because of a fear of failure and being judged," says Geoffry Loane. "Monitoring should be oriented to supporting internal evaluation and development, not external audit. Nevertheless, fifteen months after an emergency response begins, we can't claim to outsiders that they should not look at us because we're in an emergency phase."[76]

Better monitoring requires proper training for local staff in particular. Knowledge by the primary implementors of agency operations of both donor and local community expectations is critical for taking full advantage of monitoring and evaluation.

The extent to which donor agencies must themselves submit to scrutiny helps dictate the degree of accountability they demand from agencies. USAID and OFDA must concern themselves with U.S. Government Accounting Office audits, with inquisitive congressional committees, with cynical media investigators and a public predisposed to suspicion about foreign aid. "U.S. vigilance is greater because of its political system," says Andrew Natsios.[77]

The more sophisticated warring parties become in manipulating aid for their ends, the more critical it is that agencies continuously evaluate the effects of their interventions. Monitoring and evaluation should be supporting agencies in pitching their aid to the correct levels and the targeted populations. Agencies need to be open to the lessons that evaluation uncovers. Donors can assist these evaluation processes as well, sometimes simply by asking questions at critical junctures. For example, soon after the humanitarian emergency erupted in Rwanda, USAID in Washington asked field staff whether their aid was benefiting any group disproportionately or unfairly. In addition, "how sustainable structures are being reinforced should be evaluated earlier on," says a food security adviser. "We need to bring in professionals with the broadest vision to review wider impacts, responsibilities, and dilemmas of the response."[78]

For monitoring and evaluation to be taken seriously by all responders to complex emergencies, the benchmarks for success must be changed. Strong consideration should be given to building monitoring and evaluation components more directly into donor grant requirements and then providing a forum in which evaluation lessons can be routinely channeled back into operational planning.

A donor official forwards additional questions that agencies must ponder when developing their monitoring and evaluation strategies: "Can monitoring approaches be standardized, thus reducing costs and the management burden on host organizations? What are the reasons for the monitoring—and how can the results be effectively utilized to foster greater accountability? Should there be joint evaluations? Mutual evaluations?" Being able to answer these and other questions will prepare agencies better for the complex challenges of complex emergencies.

Commandment 8: Integrate Human Rights Monitoring, Advocacy, and Capacity-Building Objectives

Unlike human rights monitoring and advocacy organizations such as Human Rights Watch and Amnesty International, most relief and development agencies' mandates do not include speaking out aggressively and publicly on human rights issues. But many of these agencies provide key information to human rights groups. Tremendous benefits would be derived from greater coordination between those that can respond publicly to particular human rights incidents and issues and those that can't. For example, MSF could withdraw from Ethiopia in 1984 or Goma ten years later and shed light on particularly egregious practices while other agencies continue to provide needed assistance, serve as witnesses, at times provide a deterrent to more severe actions, and quietly channel information to human rights organizations. Over time, all agencies must make cost-benefit analyses of their interventions: "If we're not helping in silence, maybe we should leave and speak out," suggests a USAID official. Clarity about mandates is essential because it frees agencies to focus on what they should be doing rather than constantly being pulled in uncomfortable directions for which they may not be qualified or prepared.

When a relief and development agency chooses consciously to actively expand its mandate into the human rights arena, it should approach its new task in a similar manner to approaching a new sector in its development work. Staff with appropriate expertise and sensitivities must be hired, existing staff must be trained, and mechanisms for coordination and reporting must be developed to avoid making mistakes that might exacerbate the local dynamics of conflict and rights abuse. In many cases, a proper assessment will determine that a conventional relief and development agency might not be equipped to take on involvement in more political areas and that wearing multiple hats in a particular context would be inappropriate or counterproductive.

Conventional human rights monitoring and advocacy are critical components of the international response to complex emergencies. In situations of divided governance, human rights can be used as a measure of legitimacy to the outside world.

Local perceptions of group and individual rights are often little understood by outsiders. Assessment of individual rights, although quite accurate in many instances, is often used to justify certain abuses. "The idea that an interest in human rights is a western import serves the interests of local violators of human rights."[79] Nevertheless, humanitarian focus on individuals' rights can ignore and undermine survival strategies based on commitment to group survival and preservation of a way of life, as among the Dinka. Aid groups should recall the UN Refugee Convention's declared right to "maintenance of culture" and consider focusing on community rather than individual rights where individuals' vulnerability stems from communal dissolution.[80]

Famine early warning must systematically incorporate the human rights surveillance that it now parallels, creating indicators of the forcible resettlements, attacks on markets, and resource thefts that are as crucial as weather monitoring. This surveillance requires trained local participants, who may be the only logistically feasible data sources in volatile, insecure, low-intensity conflicts.[81]

There is often tension between protection and assistance, with the former sacrificed to prioritize the latter. Protection mandates in practice have been hollow. UNAMIR failed in its mandate to protect internal displacees in the Kibeho massacres by the Rwandan Patriotic Army (RPA) troops of April 1995. MSF and others urge expanding the UN peacekeeping law and definition of self-defense to include defending protected sites and groups.[82] Defying extreme danger, the ICRC carried out its protection mandate in Rwanda between April and July 1994.

The Rwandan government pressured the UN into leaving protection of the Rwandan populace out of the June 1995 renewal of UNAMIR's mandate. The renewal reduced the peacekeeping force and shifted its focus to confidence building despite the fragile situation in Rwanda and the Rwandan government's unclear ability to control border incursions and militia activity.[83] By the end of 1995, UNAMIR's mission was terminated.

The UN human rights monitoring mission in Rwanda had not standardized its information gathering methods as of mid-1995. With a new administrative team in place by September 1995, there were plans to finally address some basic coordination and information issues as well as to develop a computer-mapping capacity where correlations could be drawn between human rights violations and troop rotation, opening of schools, and other factors that might increase or decrease the incidence of violations.

An important indirect role for donor agencies and governments ought to be publicizing and dissuading human rights abuses, particularly such indirect ones as gross labor exploitation and market distortion in the shadow of potential violence as well as the use of food as a weapon of war.[84]

Prioritizing and coordinating human rights tasks is key. In most emergencies, human rights groups publicize abuses and make extraordinary demands of warring factions that have no hope of being realized. Relief and development agencies usually do not incorporate human rights objectives into their programming. Human rights components are often missing in the mandates of peacekeeping forces, as they were in UNITAF, UNOSOM, and pregenocide UNAMIR.

One donor official observes, "Human rights is becoming a bigger and bigger part of our response. Bernard Kouchner says the European Union should send hundreds of monitors to emergency situations; this is much cheaper than sending troops." The current

standoff over the return of the Rwandan refugees is largely dependent on the refugees' perceptions of the human rights situation they
will face upon their return.

The SPLA held its own human rights workshop in the quest to
imbue principles of respect for rights into its command structure.
Serious discussions were held regarding the human rights record of
the SPLA and some of the values inherent in military life. Specifically,
the slogan "my food comes from the barrel of a gun" was discussed
at length. Although tremendous strides have been made in the SPLA
in terms of public acknowledgment of abuses, Col. John Garang, the
commander-in-chief of the SPLA, claims that he doesn't control his
officers in terms of how they treat local populations. The evasion of
responsibility by commanders is thus institutionalized right from the
top. As discussed in the previous section, engagement on a day-to-
day basis by the humanitarian community is critical in inculcating a
sense of responsibility on the part of commanders.

A discussion paper for UNICEF by Iain Levine urges active protection of children in emergencies, grounded in the Convention on
the Rights of the Child and international humanitarian law and principles. Complex emergencies are breaking down the former dichotomy between human rights as political critique and humanitarian aid
as apolitical charity as massive, systematic rights abuses force donors
to confront the "sheer inadequacy of providing goods and services
without seeking to protect rights" or to make the latter a fundamental aspect of assistance.[85]

The paper notes that relief workers must proactively advocate
and educate about rights and systematically document violations.
Nationals should provide education—to defuse charges of imposing
foreign values—that should reach the following: relief staff; local
government, rebel, military, NGO, church, and traditional leaders;
and women's groups and influential professionals. Documenting
violations requires determining what types to address and not
address and how and to whom to report them (e.g., in country or
through an international office).[86]

Often human rights groups and humanitarian organizations do
not sufficiently address the importance of building indigenous capacities to deal with abuses in a society. African Rights presents a different model of what human rights organizations might do. Its Nuba
Mountains (Sudan) work provides an example. There, it has supported a local human rights monitoring system and human rights
education programs and is supporting the development of a judiciary. "This approach is based on the belief that it is inappropriate to
advocate an 'international rescue' without developing a local capaci-

ty that can ensure that it is the Nuba themselves, and not the international agencies, that dictate the priorities," writes Alex de Waal. "We also think that it is inappropriate to separate human rights from humanitarian action, and have tried to integrate them within one program."[87] It remains to be seen whether this model is viable only in cross-border operations in defiance of sovereignty or whether these kinds of initiatives can be undertaken in the context of a negotiated access framework.

Commandment 9: Coordinate at All Levels

In order to fully address aid's role in sustaining conflict, agencies and donors must enhance coordination, communication, and decision-making chains of command, both within a country and regionally. The role of the UN's DHA should be revamped and its coordination role in the field, which currently varies from emergency to emergency, clarified. UN agencies responding to emergencies—UNICEF, UNHCR, UNDP, and WFP—must eventually be reined in by the Secretariat and better coordinated, most logically by DHA. Lines of authority within the UN system should be clarified, and the number of senior decisionmaking officials should be reduced. Individual donors must improve their own interagency coordination within their governments as well, and donor roundtables and consultative groups should include relief activities in their discussions. Agencies within an individual country's aid apparatus need to cooperate in jointly reviewing proposals and evaluating projects.

At the outset of major emergencies (preferably *before* if early warning systems are utilized and heeded) that draw dozens of agencies to the scene, coordination over a rational division of responsibilities is critical in avoiding manipulation by warring factions over the placement of agency resources and other unintended consequences of large-scale humanitarian responses. Donors, DHA, and veteran agencies should all strive to increase the opportunities for coordination, to come to a consensus on a division of labor, and to facilitate discussion on program areas. Even if only the major agencies can agree on a coordination mechanism, their leadership by example can influence others.

Rudy von Bernuth of the International Council of Voluntary Agencies has suggested that in their RFPs, donors could ask agencies to submit their organizational policies on field coordination mechanisms and the instructions regarding coordination that they send to the field. Unlike a heavy-handed mandate, this approach would encourage agencies to more seriously integrate field coordination into their planning processes. In 1995, InterAction, the U.S. consortium of NGOs, is asking agencies to submit their board resolutions on the Red Cross Code of Conduct or any other code in order to stimulate further thought and action on coordination and standards.

By early 1996, InterAction had moved further. Its NGO Field Cooperation Protocol Working Group had drafted a protocol committing signatories to instruct their representatives engaged in emergency response to consult with other NGOs on a wide variety of issues. Under the protocol, consensus would be sought on the following: relations with local authorities, local employment practices, local leasing and contracting, media relations, relations with indigenous NGOs, security arrangements, division of labor, information sharing on project selection, and adoption of socioeconomic program approaches.[88]

Coordination is often hindered by hiring patterns. When an agency takes overall lead responsibility in an emergency response (such as OLS in Sudan), that agency often hires sectoral specialists to coordinate sectoral responses rather than hiring coordinators per se. Hiring sectoral specialists makes sense from a technical point of view, but they need training to enable them to fulfill the multiple demands that coordination requires.

A major area that requires coordination is information gathering. The framework provided by the Greater Horn of Africa Initiative could be useful in improving the communication lines throughout that region, in turn assisting in the coordination of regional planning.

With little clarity about security and judicial processes in Rwanda, most (new-case) refugees in Zaire and Tanzania are unwilling to return. "The coordination among donors is pitiful," charges an agency official. "If donors would coordinate their aid in addressing [degrees of culpability], they could make a major impact." The lack of coordination in response to the Kibeho massacre is another case in point of lack of donor collaboration to achieve agreed-upon purposes, as is a failure to coordinate the response to internally displaced persons. "DHA in Rwanda has no resources and works by month-to-month contracts," says one donor official. "They should have had technical people to help coordinate each sector." One bright spot was the coordination role played by Charles Petrie of DHA, who has earned accolades from agency personnel. "Petrie was a real catalyst for international NGOs, local NGOs, and the government," recalls an agency country director. "People were willing to come together."[89]

Near the end of the existence of the United Nations Rwandan Emergency Office (UNREO), the coordinating body began to work with UNDP to establish a Disaster Management Team to do joint assessments and contingency planning with the government of Rwanda and NGOs. Earlier, the U.S. OFDA DART managed the Civil Military Operations Center, which coordinated humanitarian agencies, OFDA, and the U.S. military.

The SACB possesses a mandate to do meaningful coordination. "The most positive aspect of the SACB is the acceptance by donors of their responsibility," says Geoffry Loane.[90] One of the most important aspects of the development of common policy through the SACB is the insulation against manipulation: "The Somalis know it exists; they can't manipulate agencies one by one," asserts a donor official. But the leadership style of the secretariat is forceful and controversial, and some agencies feel it is inappropriate. Furthermore, the effectiveness of the SACB's coordination suffered at the end of 1994 when the decisionmaking authority was moved from Nairobi to Geneva. Some agency personnel also charge that the SACB meetings are merely procedural, and "there is very little discussion about the substance of the needs of Somalia," says one agency consultant. The same charge is made by other agency managers regarding the donor roundtable in Rwanda.

The experiences in Rwanda and Somalia also point to the need for more coordination in the development of strategy among the political, military, and humanitarian components of the response. The humanitarian representatives are often marginalized in important policy decisions, which often leads to warped priorities bearing little resemblance to the original motivations prompting intervention.

In 1994, OLS initiated regular meetings to coordinate specific aspects of the humanitarian response in southern Sudan. OLS is attempting to develop a practice in which all agencies, even those not in OLS, would broadly agree on southern Sudanese food aid requirements lest the warring parties play agencies off against each other.[91]

Although OLS has the official role of coordinating agencies in southern Sudan, twelve NGOs have created an NGO forum to address the gaps in coordination that they perceive to be inhibiting performance and to open dialogue with donors. The group supports OLS and the access it provides as well as the rehabilitative strategy and a common NGO stance regarding abuses of humanitarian assistance. "NGOs want to meet regularly with donors to sensitize them to the difficulties of being in the field in a war zone," states an NGO official.

Also in Sudan, both SEOC and the CART operation in Juba have failed to clarify roles and responsibilities in complex operations, which should urge donors to attend to coordination and accountability of such local operations. Moreover, donors must coordinate among themselves to pressure the government to allow better access and stop manipulating relief agencies—a role that a local consortium cannot fill.[92]

Coordinating on a regional level is key as well. Exchanging information among agencies between countries and between refugee camps and countries of origin must be a task more consciously undertaken. Donors should take some responsibility for coordination at this level. UNHCR is a key UN agency in regional planning and coordination. CARE is developing a regional response plan for the Great Lakes Region, and MSF—H has spearheaded a regional coordination exercise for that region to improve information flow.

On issues that require coordination, an open, direct, immediate chain of command is invaluable. "However unfashionable they may be in management theory," writes Natsios, "simple and lean hierarchical organizations are needed in complex emergencies."[93]

Commandment 10: Prioritize Engagement and Capacity Building with Authorities and Civil Institutions

Engagement and capacity building are perhaps the most important components of a strategy of minimizing aid's sustenance of conflict. Engagement and capacity building are key concepts in most attempts to operationalize humanitarian principles. Engagement can be defined as actively advocating particular principles with authorities as well as consulting with them on these issues and building where appropriate on their views. One donor official cautioned against excessive sanctimony: "I have a problem with *our* engaging *them*, particularly when we are obliterating our own public welfare responsibilities in the North."

Regarding capacity building, the Providence Principles state, "Humanitarian assistance should enhance, not supplant, local responses." The Mohonk Criteria add, "Humanitarian assistance should strengthen the efforts of local governmental and non-governmental organizations to relieve suffering and build self-reliance." And the Red Cross and NGO Code of Conduct summarizes, "Humanitarian assistance should build on local responses."[94] Engagement and capacity building can play major roles in minimizing the sustenance of conflict, though African Rights cautions against aid agency involvement in capacity building: "The central problem is that aid delivery and civil institution-building are two very different tasks, and that the agencies' priority for delivering aid distorts their attempts to shape civil institutions."[95]

Engaging Authorities on Their Public Welfare Responsibilities

According to the Geneva Conventions, the primary responsibility for the welfare of a civilian population is with the authority of that area, which is the first line of response. Humanitarian agencies and donors can be a positive influence in encouraging the fulfillment of these responsibilities. Even if it's lip service, agencies have a duty to challenge authorities on their public welfare responsibilities.

Aid providers should also engage local communities on their commitment to addressing the needs of their most vulnerable members. According to a donor official, "Somali society should help its vulnerable groups. The onus of responsibility must be thrown on the community. We can give them ideas, but they should construct their social welfare approaches." Aid providers should then support these local decisions and initiatives.

External engagement and solidarity (tough-minded, demanding accountability and reciprocity) are necessary for effective conflict transformation. By day-to-day engagement of authorities, agencies must strive to contribute to moving these authorities from predatory relations with vulnerable populations to relationships built on reciprocity. Although the chances for success are low and the conflicts will not end through this investment of diplomatic capital, any small buttressing of the rebuilding of internal social relations is critical.

Engagement for humanitarian space should also be a major priority. Checkpoints, shakedowns, searches, and other abuses of humanitarian intent must be addressed constantly. "We have to get on top of this or we'll have to pay our way in, which we'll never be able to afford," warns a regional director of an agency.

"Day-to-day engagement of authorities should be the priority," asserts one NGO country director. Because of the huge impact agencies and the resources they bring in can have, there is major untapped potential in terms of the effect that agencies can have on the evolution of authorities. The soldiers, officers, and bureaucrats in the field must be engaged as well. "The discussions in [capital cities] on public welfare and humanitarian ethics are meaningless unless they are dealt with at the village level," says Gordon Wagner, a former OFDA official.[96]

The success of interventions is largely determined by the nature of the controlling authorities' relationship with civilian populations. This point is usually overlooked, ignored, or little understood in most analyses of interventions, but in the long run it is perhaps the single most important lesson of all the intervention experience in the Horn. The most critical experience in this regard is that of Ethiopia and Eritrea during their long wars. What are the detailed lessons?

At their very foundational core, as Duffield and Prendergast have elaborated, the EPLF and TPLF developed the political practice of linking mass mobilization with the provision of public welfare. The EPLF and TPLF provided the bulk of public welfare assistance in areas under their control until the mid-1980s as part of their political practice. Significant cross-border assistance didn't occur until the conflict had raged for twenty-five years in Eritrea and a decade in Tigray. The internationally donated cross-border aid—channeled through ERA and REST via Sudan—after 1985 greatly contributed to containing widespread food insecurity.[97]

The efficiency of the integrated and participatory relief systems of ERA and REST meant that Eritreans and Tigrayans did far more with the relatively little international assistance that they received than would have been possible using conventional relief practices. The ultimate effectiveness of ERA and REST was rooted in their decentralized and participatory welfare structures; in contrast with the more typical centralized, nonparticipatory structures that operated in Ethiopian government areas. A key component of the cross-border operation was that people were urged and assisted to stay in their home areas to maximize production. Secondary distributions and aggressive resettlement were also key strategic elements of the humanitarian programs of ERA and REST.

All externally provided resources went directly to support indigenous political and humanitarian structures, which had a huge impact on building local capacity. Neither the EPLF nor TPLF allowed international NGOs to operate during the 1980s (with the exception of ICRC, briefly), so all implementation was done by ERA and REST and their community-level structures. The fronts viewed their own approach (marked by community organizing and mobilizing combined with military advance and consolidation) as far superior to one that ceded control to international agencies.

The following strategies pursued by the EPLF and TPLF were critical in building the capacity and institutional autonomy of ERA and REST and in building the foundation for self-reliance and democratic development in front-held areas during the war: women's rights and production opportunities were expanded dramatically by the EPLF and TPLF; building local capacity to manage emergencies was prioritized by NGO consortiums, ERA, REST, and the fronts themselves; the EPLF and TPLF guaranteed institutional autonomy to ERA and REST and for the most part stuck to this guarantee throughout the war; local structures were developed to support production (e.g., agricultural extension, credit, and food for work for conservation projects); mobile skill building—primary health care, education, and training—always received great stress; and internal trade, especially in Tigray, was promoted.

As the experience with ERA and REST shows, widespread participatory processes established by in-country authorities were critical in establishing an effective operation. The relationship between authorities and populations under their control must be examined by aid providers. When predation is the norm, new relationships and aid processes must be constructed. Effective relief often requires institutional reform of local political forces.

ERA and REST have created an unrealistic yardstick against which other indigenous NGOs have since been judged. For example, without a public welfare mandate for the SPLA, the SRRA is incapable of replicating the effectiveness of ERA and REST, especially as donors focus on the SRRA only as they press for institutional autonomy for the SRRA, or press for its reform, but only rarely engage regarding the broader reform of the movement.

Both the EPLF and TPLF prioritized reciprocal relations with Eritrean and Tigrayan peoples and practiced a form of humanitarian politics that gave priority to distributing food and services to the people. Both developed the political practice of linking mass mobilization with public welfare provision. Their experience cannot be replicated elsewhere unless the local controlling authorities in other places where intervention may be called for appreciate this fundamental ideology.

The antithesis of these organizing principles can be found throughout the rest of the region—mass mobilization by coercion (Sudan) or by the promise of booty from banditry and extortion (Somalia) and no internal public welfare mandates or reciprocity with local populations under the control (or rather domination) of local or regional authorities. Quite obviously, where there are abusive authorities, there is the consistent abuse of aid. Governments, rebel organizations, and militia groups who fit this description abound throughout the Horn. At present there is little political engagement of the military leadership of any of these authority structures.

Engagement of these authorities can take many forms. As mentioned earlier, when it is done it is usually through the humanitarian wings of rebel movements, not military leaders. For local capacity building to succeed fully, these military authorities must be constantly diplomatically engaged politically, not only on the need for freedom and space at the local level but also on the development of reciprocal relationships with their own people.

This area is where the question of donors placing conditions on humanitarian aid becomes relevant (to be covered in more detail later). Conditions requiring good governance and reciprocity have by-products beyond their direct intentions; the EPLF and TPLF arguably showed that participatory processes and reciprocity were critical in gaining and maintaining the local support necessary to succeed in their broader political and military objectives.

In the Horn, the whole concept of good governance on the part of the broad range of controlling authorities in the region is aggravated and complicated by the consistent prioritizing of food aid over nonfood aid. Food aid is often much more easily manipulated and abused than nonfood aid: Food aid helps feed war economies in the region, and dependence benefits military movements as they tax or divert relief inputs.

More timely and knowledgeable responses allow for more flexibility in the nonfood response. Agricultural, veterinary, and other nonfood interventions help reinforce local subsistence and trade, which in turn reinforce self-reliance and livelihood preservation, which thereby reinforce the preservation of cultures, many of which are in jeopardy throughout the region. Nonfood aid and the corresponding emphasis on livelihoods indirectly reinforces the authority of nonmilitary segments of the local elite, and providing this kind of aid reinforces strategies of engagement on reciprocity.

Encouragingly, the ratios of nonfood to food aid have improved dramatically in both Somalia and southern Sudan, and the current experimentation in employment-based safety nets in Ethiopia will yield important lessons for other chronic emergency interventions.

Agency efforts at capacity building in the Horn—one way to address the way aid is used on the ground—are minuscule and usually come years after the interventions have begun and habits have been internalized. There is no agency or mechanism formally charged with building local capacity, so efforts are extremely erratic. Again, the EPLF and TPLF were unique in their political philosophy of developing the capacity of local communities to manage emergencies. In Somalia, local NGOs have been the prime target of capacity building, but with little attempt at standardization. These efforts have also been undermined by monetization of little-monitored projects and insufficient resources and patience for training. In Sudan, capacity-building efforts have largely been through the humanitarian arms of the rebel movements and more recently though a handful of local NGOs, mostly "locally based" in Nairobi. More care and effort must go into strengthening the political and social structures and religious organizations of civil society at the local level, to assist the development of a popular alternative to predatory militia groups.

Engagement requires coordination among all actors. "The embassies have to be involved, and donors have to be willing to follow up with some resource injection" as a carrot, offers Matthew Bryden.[98] For example, some donors suggest that repatriation be a condition for more assistance to the government of Rwanda but then are sometimes unwilling to confront (and then support) that government on essential prerequisites for repatriation. "Approaching these thorny issues solely from a humanitarian perspective is problematic," cautions Iain Levine of OLS. "Participation and accountability are deeply political."[99]

Donor agencies occasionally play hardball with authorities. Andrew Natsios says that when he was OFDA director, he went to the Mozambican government and demanded that it repay the U.S. government for diverted commodities.[100] Sometimes, though, the hardball is misdirected. After a field visit to southern Sudan by Nan Borton, OFDA's current director, during which a major diversion occurred, OFDA cut off funds for the capacity-building project for the SRRA and RASS administered by OLS. "To reduce support for capacity building when the army [SPLA] screws up seems aimed at the wrong target," one donor official confided.

"Whatever reforms are made by the SPLA result from donor pressures," claims a longtime observer of southern Sudan. "The SPLA is walking a fine line; they're not committed either way." Part of the rationale for the newly created NGO coordination mechanism in southern Sudan is to facilitate unified and direct engagement with the SRRA. "Donors should be sensitive to the unique operating conditions and give more space for NGO access," asserts Ted Chaiban of CRS.[101]

Capacity Building with Authorities

Capable, responsive governance and administration is a critical element in developing capacity to prevent conflict. There is great variation in the way different international agencies address the issue of capacity building and the engagement of local authorities. For some, capacitation is an early priority; for others, maintaining control and circumventing authority are preferable. NGO circumvention of authorities has become a major issue in the Horn, especially in areas where governments or authorities believe that NGOs should not be replacing authorities in their capacities as planners, assessors, implementors, and evaluators.

Some agencies' vision of capacity building goes no further than handing out cash to relief wings of rebel organizations. The SEOC has given large amounts of inadequately monitored money to the SRRA in Nairobi. The ERD did the same with the ERA and REST in Ethiopia, although with greater certainty that the end result would have humanitarian ramifications.

If a decision is made by an agency or agency consortium to support a capacity-building agenda, then these players must create the capacity within themselves to carry out such an agenda responsibly. Sycophantic solidarity is a damaging substitute for accountable engagement or principled advocacy because agencies doing the former make the legitimate work of those doing the latter much more difficult.

A long-term vision is needed to create a constructive framework for capacity building. The need for such a framework is pronounced in the Greater Horn because of the lack of trained personnel, the main constraint in most of the humanitarian wings and civil structures of authorities in the region. But a principal failure of many agencies is that they do not build up their own capacity to in turn build the capacity of authorities in their locale. This problem requires a staffing response; someone should be hired early on in an emergency to address capacity-building questions across the board. "There is an amazing lack of professionalism in project planning and management in the humanitarian field," bemoans Helge Rohn of Norwegian People's Aid.[102]

Training done by more experienced professionals within the region holds even more promise for success. "We can learn a great deal from ERA and REST," claims a top SRRA official. This initiative has moved forward during 1995. The local civil administration mechanisms being forged by the SPLA could also benefit from idea sharing and training by ERA and REST personnel. (Along these lines, the National Resistance Movement [NRM] in Uganda would be in a position to advise on the development of the Sudan People's Liberation Movement [SPLM] Village Liberation Council strategy of local governance.) Local-level capacity building in the field is a necessary companion to training and engagement of top officials in any authority structure.

Good Governance.   One objective of capacity building in divided or collapsed societies is the support of grassroots governance. This can be viewed as a tool of preventive diplomacy. Governance is often a source of conflict at the national level *and* the local level, and providing training and other support can enhance the professionalism of local authority, which in turn can help increase the stake of local populations in their local representation, which can affect local stability. Both local communities and donors need to give a great deal of thought to what functions of a local authority are sustainable without major external financing and adapt to a more self-reliant future reality. For example, in some areas of northern Kenya, communities have set up their own health insurance schemes. In many war-torn communities in the Horn, water systems and animal health services are established and privatized.

Assisting with the development of nonrapacious revenue-generating mechanisms increases the self-reliance of local community governments. In theory, when local authorities are financially supported by their communities, those authorities will be more responsive to the needs of their constituents. And reciprocity is critical in reducing the abuse of externally provided aid.

For example, in Somalia UNOSOM put money into local administration but thought nothing of the transition beyond UNOSOM period. The EU is proposing food for work for district councils and other local-authority functionaries—police, medical staff, prison workers—but other donors have balked. Again, questions of sustainability are relevant. If certain functions of government extant during the past two decades are not supportable by the current resource base, should outsiders help set them up and support them for a time, with no sustainability guarantees?

To have a tax base that can eventually finance community social service systems beyond kinship, wealth creation must occur. This approach requires an examination of potential private sector, community development initiatives that can bring a profit to a community, which an authority providing certain services can tax: for example, surplus agricultural products in Rwanda, livestock trade in southern Sudan, or port development in Somalia. These kinds of sequential connections need to be thought through by local communities in partnership with international agencies. Avoiding past patterns of exploitation will be particularly challenging.

Another approach to capacity building in divided or collapsed states is sectoral. Capacity building must be integrated into the planning processes of each sectoral response to emergencies: food security, water, sanitation, health, veterinary services, and so on. Training and the encouragement of responsibility-taking by local authorities should be a part of all responses. If an objective of capacity building is to assist communities in managing the response to chronic crisis, then this approach makes eminent sense. For example, in anticipation of the re-creation of a collapsed health service, capacity building can take the form of training medical personnel, standardizing health guidelines, and discussing how to restructure health provision in a manner relevant to limited-resource, highly unstable environments. "This is the best long-term investment in accountability," claims a donor official in Ethiopia. "We should always engage the lowest-level authority structure to develop the constituency for the respect for humanitarian principles."

One of the most important elements of a capacity-building strategy is for agencies not to continue a local "brain drain" by hiring the best and brightest away from their indigenous institutions or governments and paying them much more in an agency setting. These parallel systems often employ the best talent for what are often externally framed sets of priorities. A donor agency representative highlights other potential drawbacks of a capacity-building strategy with local authorities:

> I have a problem with capacity building in "failed state" environments. There are no obvious counterparts (even elders and religious leaders are sometimes suspect and/or impotent). We can end up doing damage by strengthening what we think are credible local structures but are instead shells (good English speakers adept in "Western ways") without substance or true constituencies. And what about the potential danger of reinforcing "Balkanization" of failed states? Take Somalia, for example. Most donors agree that in the absence of a national government we should be focusing on and strengthening regional and local administrative structures. Are we sure we know what we're doing? Will we succeed in strengthening these local structures to the extent that they have even *less* chance of uniting in one national structure? Are we, by working for regional and local, working against national?
> *Capacity building* is a term loosely used. There are big differences between building capacity at the grassroots, project-oriented, usually sectoral level and building capacity at the administrative and management level. The different levels of capacity building warrant different strategies and approaches.

Two specific examples of capacity building with authorities follow:

District Councils in Somalia.[103]   An attempt to re-create civil administrative authorities in a situation of state collapse took place in Somalia when the Swedish Life and Peace Institute and UNOSOM attempted to implement an agreement among the factions to allow the creation of district councils. The Addis Ababa peace agreement staked out a "two-track" approach to peace in Somalia that was supposed to address grassroots peacemaking with warlord accommodation on parallel tracks. The district councils were envisioned as the lowest level of local administration in the reconstitution of the Somali state.

The Life and Peace Institute has district council training centers in Garowe, Jowhar, and Baidoa, with international trainers paired with Somali counterparts. District councilors undergo roughly a week of training in administration and management. Training sessions usually include council members from several different locations, stimulating cross-communal interchange and communication. A requirement was agreed to by the factions at the Addis Ababa conference that a woman must be on the district council in every location.

The district councils are a new development in Somali political structure building and arguably allow a new approach to participation. They are nevertheless a foreign entity whose structure was determined externally. In some places, the new form of participation may work, and communities may come to own their councils. But in others, parallel structures have already formed and the district council has been marginalized and rejected as an external imposition. In still others, the councils threatened existing interests and have for that reason been sidelined.[104]

UNOSOM's hasty implementation of the district councils has also undermined their validity. At the time of elections in many places, displacement was too great to allow truly representative institutions. "We are disenfranchising people," observes a Somali activist.

Mark Bradbury attributes what he sees as the district councils' failure to UNOSOM's bureaucratic centralism:

> Constituted by governments, its mandate is to establish centralized governmental structures, albeit with some emphasis on decentralized regional structures. Centralized government is the very thing that many Somalis have been fighting against. As implemented by the UN, approaches to peace-making in Somalia reveal the dangers of trying to impose an outside solution to the Somali conflict.[105]

Bradbury's research identified other concerns, including:

- the legitimacy of the districts;
- the fairness and extent of external manipulation of the council elections by officials including UNOSOM Political Affairs Director Leonard Kapungo;
- the current councils' questionable representativeness, given mass displacement;
- the replacement of existing local governmental structures;
- the tokenism of the one-woman requirement;

- the uncertainty over council jurisdiction and authority;
- the lack of resources;
- the inadequate time both for UNOSOM to form the councils and for training councilors (less than a week); and
- the uncertainty of the role of elders in forming the councils.

In some locations, such as Bardera, district councils grossly over-represent the dominant subclan of that locale, and training sessions for those councils arguably buttress the legitimacy of such imbalances.

Even more fundamental are questions about the sense of ownership that communities have over these district councils. In Bay and Bakool (before Aidid's September 1995 invasion of Baidoa), the creation of a clan-based Supreme Council had rendered the local district councils largely irrelevant, as has the resumption of elder authority in Absame areas of the Juba Valley. "The Digil-Mirifle have developed a protective structure based on human affinities," says one observer. "The sense of communal responsibility is toward the clan. That's what needs to be mobilized."

"Clan-based institutions offer more credible partners than the district councils," asserts one diplomat. "Some clan-based systems and some district councils will likely emerge as credible authorities. In reality, the district councils that work are essentially clan based and not trying to reconcile hostile communities." Where district councils do remain, they are being reoriented and reconstituted by the true authority structure of the area.

For example, in Kismayu the district council is largely a formality, a functionary for the military and elder-authority structure. There is no organization of public services such as health or sanitation. The education system is completely privatized and includes no involvement of the council.

The Supreme Council in the Digil-Mirifle areas was envisioned as the civil administration for Bay and Bakool (at least until Aidid's invasion). A compelling argument existed, before Aidid's intervention, to work through the council, building its capacity and constantly challenging it on good-governance issues. Some—such as Andrew Natsios—have even suggested that security aid should have been provided to the Digil-Mirifle leaders for their self-defense.

Operation Lifeline Sudan.[106]   OLS began its most concerted capacity-building program with the SRRA—and later RASS—in 1993. The initial objective was to build the capacity of these organizations for delivering humanitarian aid. The results so far are widely debated.

"This is the first time that values, principles, and structures which undergird the movements were discussed," points out a former donor official. A contrary view is expressed by another donor official: "The capacity-building program has only succeeded in bolstering the mafiosos. RASS and SRRA were made the official counterparts of OLS. They were grossly empowered."

African Rights points out that the humanitarian space that the OLS capacity-building program in southern Sudan promoted has actually made some room for dialogue among southerners, creating a "locus of liberalism in Southern Sudanese political society, [attracting] highly-educated and motivated individuals. Perhaps most important, it has also offered a measure of protection to Southerners who have wanted to air dissenting opinions." African Rights concludes that although peace and reconciliation was a quiet agenda of the OLS capacity-building initiative, cooperation between opposing factions was largely limited to Nairobi and did not trickle down to the field level. Similarly, capacity building of Sudanese NGOs enabled some talented individual Sudanese to build stronger constituencies in the south rooted in humanitarian action and political liberalism, but without international backing, their vulnerability is very high.[107]

Going beyond its original mandate, OLS held a workshop in 1995 that included many administrators and governors from the field. The civil administrators attending this workshop challenged the SRRA, saying that diversion of humanitarian supplies by the SPLA takes resources away from their communities. "The SRRA finally acknowledged this and moved things forward," notes a former UN official.

The deep-seated problems in southern Sudan require more than material aid, including follow-up and encouragement of a 1994 SPLM announcement of a "New Sudan" structure to empower and separate civil authorities from the military and increase democratic space for civil society.[108] Based partially on the Eritrean and Ethiopian models, the National Liberation Council (NLC) of the SPLM has recognized the importance of building structures that give authority to the people in southern Sudan. Thus, the NLC is drafting legislation to define the function, composition, and basis of representation for the liberation councils, which now exist from the village level up to the regional level.[109]

Building on this vision, agencies and donors might better serve long-term capacity-building objectives by more directly focusing on and engaging the nascent village liberation councils and SPLM structures where possible as well as the chiefs, churches, local community groups, and other elements of nonmilitary society. The SRRA and

RASS by contrast have some paper authority over line departments, but they are usually not plugged into the system at the local level. In southern Sudan, civil society is healthiest at the grassroots level. Any efforts expended building externally driven systems above this level is a diversion from real grassroots participation in rehabilitation and reconstruction. Much of the donors' engagement with the SPLM and SSIM should be over precisely this point: the need for creative space at the local level for community organizations and representatives and the philosophy that undergirds the civilianization of the movements.[110]

The UN umbrella of OLS makes it structurally unable to convene an aggressive strategy of engagement of the SPLM and SSIM on principles and practice. A group outside OLS—with firm, united donor support—might more easily address these fundamental issues with the movements. Neighboring countries have tremendous experience that could be shared formally and informally. Similarly, churches with experience in liberation struggles (Philippines, El Salvador, and South Africa) could be pulled in to engage the Sudanese churches on their long-term political and spiritual role.

Other Examples. In Rwanda, USAID supported an agenda that aimed to build up the government as quickly as possible after the RPF's assumption of power. The agency provided vehicles, computers, and other inputs to the various line ministries, including a half-million dollars for each of eight key ministries.

In Ethiopia, UNDP is supporting the building of capacity of *woreda* (district) councils to undertake food security, human resources and natural resources management, and disaster prevention. But these councils can play other roles. "*Woreda* councils are very weak in terms of implementing programs but can do conflict resolution," says Constantinos Berhe of LEM Ethiopia.[111]

Also in Ethiopia, the government has developed a National Program for Disaster Prevention, Preparedness and Mitigation. The objective of the program is to increase communities' ability to withstand emergencies through information management, improved preparedness, and stress on household food security. To support this goal, development-oriented employment safety nets are being constructed to replace food handouts. Community adaptation to chronic emergencies is critical in creating the will and capacity for reconciliation.

It is important to sound a note of restraint at this juncture. There are situations in which it is inappropriate to build official capacity, especially when such building strengthens repressive structures.

Capacity Building of Civil Society

William Zartman of Johns Hopkins University identifies the under-recognized phenomenon of civil society's resilience, even ability to thrive, during state collapse: It often cannot fill, and avoids, the national vacuum but vigorously responds to local problems. This situation gives those who would reconstruct society more opportunity to (re)build civil society—which requires open space—than the state—which requires structures.[112] External programs that invest in developing local people and organizations adapt best to future crises.[113]

In the context of emergency programming, there are many opportunities to support indigenous nongovernmental forms of social organization. In every society, there are traditional mechanisms of kinship and self-help that are often the primary contributors to a community's survival in the context of a complex emergency. "Supporting civil organizations represents development theory in practice, transported back to the rehabilitative phase," suggests an NGO manager in Rwanda.[114] Even in the structure of food distribution, promoting alternative representation (women's groups, technical committees, traditional social networks) can build local capacity and create an alternative to the military structures. "International NGOs have a big role to play in empowering dispossessed elements," points out Leenco Lata of Ethiopia. "Aid should continuously be reevaluated to see how external involvement can support empowerment."[115] Another adviser to international agencies in Ethiopia is more adamant: "Let bilateral aid support local administrations. International NGOs should support civil society and indigenous NGOs, not state structures."[116]

Mary Anderson outlines further rationales for making capacity building a central part of emergency response:

> Education, skills, and general know-how are capacities that, when applied to the physical resources of land, tools, seeds and equipment, affect people's productivity. Family and community structures through which people gain both physical and psychological support often make the difference as to who suffers most—and least—in emergencies. People's experiences in decision-making and management affect their sense of efficacy and control and also have an important effect on productivity in normal times and on survival during emergencies.[117]

But for many authorities, indigenous organizations represent a threat to bases of power and fund-raising, which makes a local capacity-building strategy extremely difficult and sometimes dangerous (for the participants) to undertake.

Furthermore, existing capacity of civil institutions throughout the Greater Horn is problematic. Although indigenous agency capacity is difficult to generalize about, Minear and Weiss of the Humanitarianism and War Project attempt to draw broad characterizations. On the positive side, they note, local NGOs are directly connected to the population and thus best suited to meet the communities' needs, offering leadership with ties to the communities; a realistic vision of the communities' future; and a natural incentive to sustain and guarantee reconstruction, development, and peace. On the negative side, these groups may be too parochial or political to effectively obtain outside resources. Their societies' customs may appear questionable to the international community.[118]

The SEOC review noted as an overarching problem of the prolonged, vicious conflict in southern Sudan the need to give donors and NGOs guidelines for dealing with the legitimate demands of pressure groups without uncritically incorporating them into the assessment process. Relief operations must establish a wider framework than that of negotiated access in order to support reconstruction of civil and professional structures, including health and education systems. Duffield et al. urge that many agencies have underestimated the resilience of the southern Sudanese subsistence economy and should focus on supporting the modern sector, which is far more vulnerable to war and necessary to southern Sudan's social and political survival. They suggest educational, professional, and vocational support.[119]

Southern Sudanese local churches' lack of organizational or managerial capacity or tradition ensured great difficulties when the SEOC collaborated with the New Sudanese Council of Churches (NSCC), especially after giving the council the sudden responsibility of identifying beneficiaries, distributing free food, and reporting the outcome. Duffield et al. note that SEOC should have considered the churches' thinly established presence among most Nilotic peoples and the likelihood that the churches, like the rebels, would devote resources foremost to consolidating their own power.[120] Much as Sudanese political and ecumenical local relief distributors competed for and demanded formulaic division of SEOC aid, so did churches compete among themselves, with those in relatively wealthy areas demanding aid from relief convoys headed to more desperate, neglected areas.[121]

The *SEOC Review* criticized the consortium's failure to build a relationship with the NSCC beyond identifying it as a distributing agent even after realizing that it couldn't fulfill that role, citing NSCC complaints that the consortium's predominant concern was "to move x number of tons of relief items." SEOC has thereby closed the door on a potential source of nonauthoritarian sociopolitical development; it must engage local partners more broadly than as aid dispensers, which allows partners to be only supplicants.[122]

CRS and OLS have both undertaken capacity-building initiatives with indigenous organizations in southern Sudan. (Other agencies have not created formal capacity-building programs, but their choice of local partners can nonetheless be key in supporting local structures. CARE's work with the road gangs and chiefs in Western Equatoria is an example, as is the support of Supraid by World Vision.) The CRS umbrella grant provides a participatory mechanism for indigenous organizations to access funding. CRS is attempting to target and develop the capacities of beneficiary organizations rather than elite intermediary groups that often lack community roots and have little concept of grassroots empowerment. "This will test the legitimacy of local organizations," predicts Ted Chaiban.[123]

The OLS initiative was a trial-and-error attempt, with many organizations chosen that did not have sufficient links with local communities. One strategy was to give the local groups a small assessment grant as a basis for judgment about their competency and performance. "One of the biggest mistakes made was not sufficiently educating international NGOs and UNICEF itself in the strategy and approach of capacity building," offers an agency official.[124]

At an OLS workshop in April 1995, many of the Sudanese NGOs themselves agreed that they should "take on a role as a lobby group on humanitarian principles with the movements. . . . OLS should provide training to Sudanese NGO staff, not only in humanitarian principles, but also in the use of drama and song as dissemination media. . . . Dissemination of humanitarian principles should take place at all levels—village, payam, county, national, in courts, cattle camps, churches, schools, mosques, etc."[125]

Understanding this trial-and-error process is key. Meaningful capacity building requires long time horizons and liberal allowances for mistakes and problems. In many places, traditions of social organization have been bludgeoned by divide-and-rule authoritarian governmental structures, creating a legacy of mistrust, lethargy, and corruption.

Supporting civil society requires patience by agencies in learning local structures of legitimate representation. For example, UNICEF now insists on talking directly with cattle-camp leaders on animal health issues in southern Sudan. If a meeting is called and the SRRA, RASS, or executive chiefs show up without the cattle-camp leaders, the meeting is canceled and rescheduled as many times as is required until the camp leaders appear. "This kind of community dialogue process can take a long time," relates Tim Leyland, the veterinary specialist of OLS. "But to really strengthen community-based organizations, in veterinary work you have to go to the cattle-camp leaders."[126] Organizers hope that the cost-recovery components of the program will soon provide the resource base for certain community social welfare initiatives, such as payment of teachers (in kind, with cattle), the building or maintenance of schools, and the digging of wells. Again, sustainability in these areas is suspect if outsiders pay for the services.

In Somalia, CARE has managed an umbrella grant and a monetization program that are able to channel grants directly to local organizations. CARE staff note a significant improvement in the capacity and accountability of some of the organizations that survived the inevitable shaking out of nonrepresentative or nonserious groups. Nevertheless, the model of working with indigenous NGOs may be misapplied to some extent in Somalia. Indigenous NGOs in most areas of the country are a false construction, a deviation from true forms of community organization. Again, it is critical to first assess what local capacity does exist and what form it takes before funding formulas are created and replicated in widely differing environments.

For example, in the Gedo Region of Somalia, some agencies such as Trocaire supported the local *xeer*, intercommunal social contracts based on traditional customs and Islamic principles. Stephen Jackson's analysis of the impact of Trocaire's work notes:

> Some small credit for the re-birth of the *xeer* can be claimed by agencies which chose to work from the earliest days with . . . what remained of the community structures. By channeling assistance through the elders, and by including them in the decision making process, they provided a much needed buttressing of the elders' waning credibility in the community. Privately, individual clan elders in Gedo will acknowledge this. There appears to be a direct consonance here between working with community structures for developmental reasons, and having a further effect in reducing conflict and building up the community's capacity to resist violence.[127]

In situations of tremendous upheaval, schools are often one of the only civil structures remaining. Support of community initiatives to re-create local elementary schools lays the groundwork for providing a voice in the community other than military imperatives.

In Rwanda, international agencies sifted through the credentials of roughly forty indigenous NGOs. Indigenous organizations were to a large degree sidelined during the postgenocide humanitarian emergency phase, so only in mid-1995 did serious engagement of local groups begin in earnest. "Part of the screening process is sincerity, not just financial viability," notes an agency official in Kigali.[128]

Capacity building of women's organizations at the local level is critical in building an alternative voice. Furthermore, introducing capacity-building objectives for women as a part of all sectoral plans is important in mainstreaming women's participation and leadership. Anisia Achieng, a coordinator of the Sudan Women's Voice for Peace, stresses the need to move beyond the elite in capital cities: "Capacity building should be targeted at the grassroots. Traditional birth attendants, widow's associations, and women's farming groups should be supported. Agencies need to assess the capacity that already exists and support that."[129]

Credit is an important form of assistance to women's organizations. In Bosaso, Somalia, UNDP set up a credit scheme to loan women $50–$100 to support or establish small businesses, such as small trade, tea shops, bicycles to move inputs, and so on. For the 235 loans made as of mid-1995, there has been a 100 percent return so far. The repayments are then channeled right back into the community.[130]

Supporting religious institutions is an important component of local capacity building. Whether a mosque or a Koranic school in Somalia or a local church group in southern Sudan or Rwanda, agencies and donors should be cognizant of the important potential religious institutions have in providing a balance to military authority in many war-torn societies.

Addressing the Trade-Off Between Control and Empowerment

One of the most important points of the Providence Principles is the imperative to not supplant local capacity. There are strong arguments for allowing greater levels of initial inefficiency on the grounds of building capacity. Institution building takes time, money, and patience. Even ICRC has changed the way it operates to more fully incorporate local involvement. "The impact of our aid is positively correlated with the degree of national involvement in the operation," observes Geoffry Loane.[131]

External control and local capacity building in emergency situations are not mutually exclusive. Agencies should attempt to maximize the latter while retaining the right of independent assessment and monitoring. For Minear and Weiss, the "tradeoffs between rapid responses and longer-term benefits may be more theoretical than real." Relief efforts that incorporate local people and institutions are more successful and need not entail major delays.[132]

Speed and accountability are two elements that need to be balanced when trying to maximize capacity building. The process is invariably slower when trying to involve local structures, but what remains after the wave of external responders is gone will be largely dependent on the level of collaboration with these local structures.

There is a great variety of opinion about the timing of capacity building. "Releasing control earlier is less costly and less disruptive," notes Willet Weeks. "The overall goal of assisting self-reliance is best served by building local mechanisms."[133] On the other hand, "it's hard to justify putting in major time to build local capacity in the emergency phase," cautions the country director of an NGO in Rwanda.

Some agency personnel worry about the level of pressure local organizations are under from their own communities. For example, according to one donor official in Ethiopia, "if the JRP was under pressure, they would feed nontargeted populations and wouldn't tell us, whereas CARE might tell us if facing a similar situation."

5

Humanitarian Aid, Conflict Prevention, and Peace Building

Chapter 4 examined strategies and approaches to emergency operations that might minimize the degree to which aid sustains conflict. This chapter addresses how aid in an emergency context might positively and proactively contribute to longer-term conflict prevention and peace building.

Humanitarian assistance is frequently (if unofficially) utilized in the service of peace processes. Natsios notes a number of ways in which diplomats utilize aid to promote their political objectives: confidence building during peace talks; undergirding democratization, stabilization, and adjustment; promoting the implementation of a peace agreement; mitigating sanctions' bite on the most vulnerable segments of society; and offering carrots in the context of negotiations.[1] For example, the major response to the southern Africa drought in 1992 had, besides the containment of famine, the corollary goals of buttressing democratic processes and structural adjustment programs throughout the region. In early 1996, the debate over whether Western donors would respond to food shortfalls in North Korea led U.S. officials to consider providing assistance in order to reward the North Korean government for complying with its 1994 promise to suspend nuclear weapons development.[2]

At the operational level, donors and aid agencies can move beyond treating the symptoms of crises and use aid to mitigate conflict and address the economic disruptions at the root of complex emergencies. NGOs and donor agencies must continue to be more flexible in removing often artificial barriers between relief and development activities.

Even beyond war zones, conflict pervades all economic development at micro and macro levels: sociocultural, over values; political, over power and decisionmaking; and economic and environmental, over resources. International organizations nonetheless generally lack institutionalized mechanisms to manage conflict.[3] Adams and Bradbury urge development organizations to abandon any implicit

belief that development would lead to political stability and to recognize that conflict pervades development, causing massive disrup-
tion and suffering, rather than appearing occasionally or as an excep-
tional.[4] Most NGOs in conflict areas lack clear, systematic principles
of their relations to conflict and its resolution, given their internally
and externally driven needs to maintain an image and ideology of
neutrality.[5] Throughout Africa's internal conflicts and complex emergencies, humanitarian agencies lopsidedly respond to the casualties
and manifestations of war, such as refugee flows, with very little
investment in peacemaking and preventing wars' expansion.[6]

Postwar reconstruction must in fact begin before war ends and
entails rebuilding infrastructure and economies, absorbing traumatic
changes in social relations (as well as demobilized fighters), and
rehabilitating every level of society—household, community, civil
group, professional association, and government—with a grasp of
social relations to avoid reinforcing inequality or deepening marginalization.[7] Adams and Bradbury also note that despite their immediate exacerbation of poverty and risk, wars in impoverished countries
can be positive agents for change. This change can be direct—when
people fight for justice and equality—or indirect, when war prompts
women's, community, and other civil groups to emerge.[8]

In this regard, Hizkias Assefa of the Nairobi Peace Initiative promotes a more expansive, proactive concept of peace that includes the
presence of social structures through which differences can be identified and worked out to the satisfaction of the parties involved and
society as a whole.[9] The Rev. Samuel Kobia, former general secretary
of Kenya's National Council of Churches, observed that "justice and
peace cannot thrive in a vacuum. There has to be a social and economic set-up within which peace can prevail."[10]

It is arguable whether—even if they revised current practice to
directly support reconciliation—agencies bring enough resources in
the context of emergencies to significantly affect national conflict-resolution processes. A less frequently contested notion is that aid—if
utilized more strategically—might be able to significantly contribute
to longer-term local processes of conflict prevention and building
peace from the bottom up.

Aid in an emergency context holds little hope for significantly
contributing to peace at the national and regional levels. But at the
subnational level, where local resources and identities are fueling
tensions, aid has great potential for addressing some of the igniting
factors. The operative principle underlying this optimism is that
given the increasing ferocity of subnational conflict, the comparative
advantage that aid agencies have in their proximity to these conflicts

on a day-to-day basis makes their engagement in laying the ground-work for eventual resolution a logical endeavor. Furthermore, the logic multiplies when the peace-building work is portrayed in functional terms. In emphasizing ways in which humanitarian assistance can foster local peace building and cooperative alternatives to conflict, Mary Anderson urges the international community to find ways to identify not merely early warning signals of imminent factional rupture and violence but early hope signals of local movements to build peace and justice.[11] Macrae and Zwi conclude that aid agencies must not merely provide resources but do so in a way that helps local institutions to rebuild if conflict resolution efforts are to lastingly facilitate recovery and forestall recurrences of violence.[12]

It is critical to conceive peace building as multilayered and multifaceted, with numerous initiatives going on at once, often with great room for enhanced coordination, networking, and strategizing. One list of efforts in southern Sudan to "empower communities around their own values, traditions, and structures" to build peace and reconciliation and protect rights and humanitarian principles includes:

- UNICEF/OLS and CRS capacity-building support to Sudanese NGOs, church groups, cooperatives, and women's groups;
- the focus on traditional values in UNICEF's humanitarian principles promotion;
- Sudan Women's Voice for Peace's grassroots mobilizations;
- the New Sudan Council of Churches Program for Peace and Justice and interpositioning;
- the Diocese of Torit's peace monitors program;
- a reconciliation conference among the Nuer ethnic group, which generated proposals to produce a convention on Nuer customary law;
- OLS's efforts with rebel relief wings to establish local committees to facilitate community involvement in aid distribution, monitoring, and rehabilitation;
- village health committees;
- the establishment of the South Sudan Law Society and its attempt to re-create a civil legal code;
- spontaneous civilian and even military grassroots peace and reconciliation efforts; and
- a traditional Pari age-group (traditional community leadership structure) takeover of the administration of Lafon in March 1995.[13]

After cataloging this wide range of NGO, church, legal, grass-roots, and traditional groups' peace mobilization and training efforts, Iain Levine of OLS proposes establishing a research and advisory forum to bring together all parties working to promote grassroots peace, reconciliation, and human rights activity.[14]

In the long run, in most places political and military leaders ultimately derive the bulk of their conscripts and support with the assent or support of business and community leaders. In Somaliland, African Rights notes, "By solving the disputes at the level of traditional social organization, the elders were able to deprive the politicians of the possibility of making war, and thus help to create the conditions of peace."[15] Some of the following strategies attempt to directly or indirectly address local problems that provide fodder for conflict.

Forging Intercommunal and Economic Links

Create Intercommunal or Cross-Line Aid Committees

Most participatory mechanisms for aid planning and distribution involve only intracommunity participation, not intercommunity cooperation. For example, the Relief Committees in southern Sudan only represent the distribution zone, which is usually a cohesive ethnic community. There is no crossing of community lines.

In areas where communities or contesting militia groups have frequently clashed and created emergency needs, agencies might facilitate the creation or support of existing intercommunal mechanisms to discuss those emergency needs. These mechanisms often already exist but are under extreme pressure. They take such diverse forms as kinship ties between neighboring communities that are activated during periods of extreme stress, local religious committees or communities that incorporate multiple groups, or border chiefs or elders whose responsibility it is to negotiate between communities in the aftermath of intercommunal conflict.

Strengthening cross-line communication may have no impact on the warleaders but perhaps will lead the peace-seeking elements of neighboring communities to see mutual interests in cooperation. With communication and cooperation partially restored, neighbors can continue to trade, graze animals, and maintain other ties even while warleaders continue to fight. Ken Menkhaus notes, "Often this simple provision of political space and a line of communication is vital to the process of conflict resolution, and can be the greatest contribution international organizations can make. . . . It focuses community attention on the very tangible benefits of cooperation and conflict resolution, rather than on peace as an abstraction."[16] These cross-line mechanisms can have extremely important preventive ramifications, providing forums to discuss rather than fight over misunderstandings and resource questions.

Border areas throughout the Great Lakes Region are logical focal points for this kind of initiative in which communication between those "outside" and those "inside" is critical for balancing perceptions. A few agencies began a series of cross-border meetings between towns inside Rwanda that face the Zairian camps. The meetings were interrupted for a time by the massacres at Kibeho, but resumed in mid-1995. Other candidates for this kind of mechanism are border areas of intercommunal conflict in southern Sudan (Duk Fadiet and Duk Faiwil between the Dinka and Nuer), Ethiopia, Somalia, and Somaliland.

In the greater Somali and Afar communities inhabiting Djibouti, Eritrea, Ethiopia, Somaliland, and Somalia, the UN is examining cross-border strategies involving resource use, trade, grazing routes, communication, and transport. Since the UNDP established guidelines regarding its response to complex emergencies, and conflict avoidance is a key element, these kinds of nontraditional cross-border planning and programming have greater latitude when being explored by UN agencies. Since these countries are all continuous recipients of emergency assistance, this regional framework should be utilized, and intercommunal planning should be a part of all emergency responses. "Going across borders to solve problems is critical," says Walid Musa.[17] Similar thinking is taking place in the Great Lakes Region, where cross-border links are strong in the movement of people, the concentration of populations, and the movement of military forces.

Entering this area of promoting intercommunal cooperation without a specific product or agenda in mind might create suspicion, leave agencies vulnerable to charges of political meddling, or generally be counterproductive. But particular interventions at the sectoral level become more sensible when seeking cross-line dialogue. Food is obviously a tool for negotiation, from OLS to the JRP in the Horn to other negotiated access agreements throughout the world. There is also room to maneuver intercommunally in areas such as animal health, education and training, water, human health, and housing.

Animal health is one area in which agencies have experimented with cross-line programming. Vaccination programs across the lines of battle are feasible because the health of their animals is critical to local communities; animals often represent their entire asset base. For example, herders of the Misseriya from southern Kordofan were not receiving veterinary services from northern Sudan and therefore wanted to be served from Akon, an area held by the SPLA. An already brisk trade between southern Kordofan and northern Bahr al-Ghazal might be further assisted by aid planners, who could provide certain inputs to the Misseriya and certain inputs to the Dinka to encourage further cooperation and perhaps help forestall an escalation of hostilities that threatens the fragile situation in that transition zone.

Animal health programming—when pursued intercommunally—provides an opportunity to operationalize matters such as codes of conduct, ground rules, or the Geneva Conventions themselves. "If raiding continues, aid will not" could be a standard condition.

Some agencies use the opportunity of animals coming together to treat people as well. Mobile health clinics and veterinarians can travel together and create further incentives for temporary intercommunal cooperation.

Education is another potential vehicle for cross-line contact. Bishop Paride Taban's Diocese of Torit has a boarding school that brings together the children of many neighboring ethnic groups in Eastern Equatoria. Although it is hoped that this programming will create increased cooperation in the present, the strategy is geared more toward creating a future atmosphere in which tomorrow's adults will have had more experience peacefully interrelating with their neighbors. Training programs, although shorter term, can also be a vehicle for bringing different perspectives and representatives of conflicting communities together on technical, joint-problem-solving grounds.

A third area for intercommunal planning is water. Bringing community water committees together to jointly plan regional drilling, maintenance, and use is a logical extension of participatory strategies. If appropriately engaged, the Regional Water Authorities in Somalia might act as mechanisms for cross-line discussion, for example.

Fourth, human health holds great potential for intercommunity cooperation. UNICEF has brokered "days of peace" and "corridors of tranquility" in order to carry out immunization programs for children. The Carter Center has used guinea-worm eradication as the logic for a temporary cessation of hostilities. The mobile clinic of CRS and the Diocese of Torit funded by the European Union Humanitarian Office (ECHO) goes across boundaries between warring parties in southern Sudan and can be a vehicle for dialogue through intercommunal planning.

Housing is yet another sector holding some promise for conscious cross-ethnic programming. In Gitarama, Rwanda, a housing reconstruction program provides Hutu locals with raw materials to build or repair housing for returning Tutsis.[18]

Promote Intercommunal Trade and Exchange

Trade and exchange mechanisms are often the most important vehicles through which communities survive times of conflict-induced scarcity and often are the most severely affected element of the food economy. Animal-grain trade, for example, is the primary survival strategy of communities throughout the Horn. Economic exchange between communities also keeps open lines of communication, which are critical for addressing misperceptions about the intentions of neighboring communities. Encouraging, supporting, and protecting these indigenous responses should be a major priority of intervening agencies.

African rural production systems have evolved coping strategies to preserve productive assets through times of stress; assets include physical resources, investments in livestock, and legitimate claims on others.[19] The 1990 and 1993 OLS assessments of southern Sudan illustrated food shortage coping strategies such as eating wild foods and small livestock as well as utilizing traditional mutual assistance networks, including long-distance intermarriage networks of access to alternate food sources in which all seek to participate, as all expect to face shortages at some time.[20]

Commercial activity is often a leading rationale for stability. Mudug in central Somalia is a continuing potential flash point because of its multiclan composition, but relative peace has held since a 1993 peace agreement because of the commercial imperative. "Mudug is the Dubai of Somalia," claims faction leader Osman Ato. "The businessmen are keeping the peace."[21] Ioan Lewis emphasizes the importance of economic incentives in consolidating peace in Somaliland during the 1991–1993 period: "Groups which had been expelled from areas of settlement by bouts of clan cleansing were anxious to return and rediscover their previous access to pasture and water and, in areas of cultivation, to arable land. The same applied in relation to town property."[22]

Organizations interested in supporting reconciliation can seek creative ways to foster interdependence rather than competition.

Exchange mechanisms are often cut off by front lines, or communities are so impoverished by chronic conflict that transporting goods back and forth becomes problematic. Means of supplying transport for locally produced and traded commodities should be explored by intervening agencies. Backhauling of goods by air, allowing trucks bringing inputs to be used for transporting local goods as well, and providing bicycles or canoes (depending on the topography) to facilitate the movement of small amounts of produce are all critical in keeping lines of cooperation open between neighboring communities whose relations may be strained by the actions of warleaders.

Cooperatives and other methods of community cooperation in some places are key actors in sustaining intercommunal exchange. Utilizing these kinds of indigenous mechanisms supports local adaptation to conflict as well as keeping lines of communication open. For example, CRS is giving money to a community cooperative in Chukudum (southern Sudan) in order to increase its purchasing power, and the cooperative is buying goods from neighboring communities, stimulating exchange among the Boya, Didinga, and Toposa, who have historically raided each other for cattle or grain. Simply knowing that these cooperative mechanisms exist is important in agency planning. For example, Rahanweyne subclans in the Bay Region are increasingly pooling their money into small, cooperative, profit-sharing businesses called *iskashis*. The profitability of these ventures and their ability to penetrate markets in Mogadishu and Bardera will greatly influence the Rahanweyne's ability to one day defend themselves against military and commercial incursions from militarily stronger and wealthier Habr Gedir and Marehan neighbors. Supporting nonindigenous forms of social organization such as local NGOs will do nothing to reduce conflict and little to reduce vulnerability in Bay Region, but perhaps supporting *iskashis* will help. The conquest of Baidoa by General Aidid in September 1995 reinforces the analysis of interdependence between Bay Region's food production and Mogadishu's markets and port. Gradually equalizing the power balance between the two neighbors is a prerequisite for nonpredatory relations.

In the Western Equatoria region of southern Sudan, cooperatives and other local producers are again selling surpluses with the help of some agencies and donors. The surplus production opens up old trade routes, some of which go across borders, which can't be completely controlled by the warleaders.

On the Ugandan side of the border, Equatorian refugees produce vegetables, seeds, and root crops for sale to other Sudanese refugees and to the Ugandan host population. There are historical links of reciprocity and ethnicity across the border that have been called upon repeatedly during the past three decades of violent conflict in both countries. Much more could be done to support the refugee populations in their production and commercial networks.[23]

Trade can be the great equalizer. Some of the conflicts in the Horn have partial roots in exclusion from trade routes. In Somaliland, perceptions of unequal access to Berbera-Jijiga trade routes fuels the Garhajis' militia in its war with the Somaliland government and its Habr Awol supporters. Agencies should at least factor this element into their humanitarian response to the displacement caused by the war to ensure that the assistance that's going into government-held areas doesn't reinforce patterns of domination and exclusion. Aid into the Lower Juba Region in Somalia also requires political savvy, as the exclusion of Ogadenis from Kismayu's political and commercial benefits enhances the likelihood of future conflict.

Address Economic Roots of Conflict

Localized conflicts that have their roots predominantly in competition over resources are obvious candidates for interventions that seek to resolve the underlying resource-driven tensions. Pressure on the food economy is a major contributing cause of cattle-raiding. "A degree of conflict is desperation-driven," says Philip O'Brien of OLS. "A secure food economy will tamp down conflict."[24] Constantinos Berhe, the director of LEM Ethiopia, notes that "conflicts are resource based at the district level, not ethnicity based. Water, grass, and land are key issues. We need to look at traditional uses of natural resources and look at how communities apply their laws to resolve conflicts."[25]

Keen and Wilson argue that using aid to reduce local violence can produce greater gains than the direct benefits of distributing commodities—and far greater gains than military strikes against perceived central villains "at the top,"[26] such as General Aidid.

The supply side of recruitment for armies and militias is often driven by failed development, as is evidenced by the recruitment by militia leaders of disenfranchised youth from Somalia's maldeveloped regions. Investment in those regions might draw some of these militia members back to their home areas. "When people are satisfied, doing business, growing crops, they will not take up arms," claims Abdi Aden Ali of Oxfam UK. "People take up arms when they see negative trends in development."[27] Low-level economic activity provides some measure of economic independence, which lessens dependence on military authorities. This result can reduce rationales for joining militias and reduce a community's dependence on aid that often cements local populations to military leaders.

For example, on the road from Boraama to Hargeisa in Somaliland, the number of checkpoints increased because people all along the road needed money to buy water from the limited number of usable water points. UNDP dug two more water holes, and the checkpoints disappeared.[28] The fighting over water points in the Bakool Region of Somalia in the spring and summer of 1995 between the Jiron and Hadame subclans was also amenable to resolution through elder negotiation backed up by limited agency resources in digging additional water points per the eventual agreement.

Environmental restoration is a key sector in which economic roots of conflict can be addressed and solutions can cut across the lines of battle. The internally displaced (IDP) camps in Rwanda—and other large-scale concentrations of people throughout the Greater Horn—have left the surrounding area stripped of its vegetative cover, accelerating erosion. Only a few agencies are addressing the environmental problems that will inevitably spawn another generation of intercommunal conflict driven by scarce resources. Furthermore, agroforestry falls outside the parameters of some donors' emergency funding.

In Sudan and Somalia, addressing the economic interests of the Baggara agropastoralists and Habr Gedir pastoralists, respectively, in their home areas would contribute to reducing the ease with which militia leaders recruit young men. The processes of maldevelopment in southern Kordofan, Sudan, and the central regions of Somalia that impoverished huge numbers of families throughout the 1980s provided a breeding ground for resentment and were easily exploited by manipulative politicians. The vast majority of externally provided resources go to the areas that these militias attack (like northern Bahr al-Ghazal, Sudan) or where they now reside as militias (such as Mogadishu) rather than their areas of origin. Thought must be given to the development of sustainable alternative livelihoods for these young men in their home areas.

As mentioned earlier, the commercial imperative often requires stability. The greater the potential for marketing—especially exporting—the more vested interest exists in defusing conflict-producing instability. The ports in Somalia hold great potential for backward peace-building linkages. The more well-functioning ports become, the higher the potential for profits, and the greater logic will exist for stability. (The problem of conquest of productive areas is not addressed, though, as the Baidoa case shows.)

Preventing Conflict and Building Peace as Explicit Objectives of Emergency Aid

Plan for Peace Building

Aware of their lack of experience, many agencies are increasingly exploring issues of peace building and reconciliation in their programming. For example, CARE held a workshop on the subject for its regional managers in the Greater Horn in early 1996, and World Vision hired a full-time adviser on reconciliation. Some agencies have a long history of peace work, including the Mennonite Central Committee and American Friends Service Committee as well as many other denominational church agencies.

In the field, various agency personnel have expressed interest in the possibility of bringing in local and international conflict-resolution experts (or those intimately familiar with the dynamics of particular conflicts) at the planning or evaluation stages to advise agencies on how to better contribute to conflict prevention and peace building. Even without such external assistance, some agencies informally introduce conflict mitigation or prevention as specific objectives in their planning processes. This objective requires checking the location, staffing, and project content for peace-building potential. Nevertheless, says peace activist Kabiru Kinyanjui of Kenya, "Most NGOs are still not incorporating peace building into their programming. Long-term concerns are usually ignored. Most are investing in relief and ignoring reconciliation. Relief is higher profile."[29] Again, however accurate, this analysis partially stems from misunderstanding or ignoring the necessary division of responsibilities that must be clarified among humanitarian, human rights, and conflict-resolution objectives. Operational agencies need not be mediators at a negotiating table (or even under a tree), but their programming should at the least not be contributing to the exacerbation of tensions and at best can be astutely addressing some of the root causes of conflict—which is the essence of peace building.

To ensure that relief and development aid reduces rather than intensifies conflicts, Adams and Bradbury recommend an approach of continual monitoring and evaluation of whether activities raise or lower the risk of conflict. They note development agencies' assistance of Rwandan community work as a potential, inadvertent source of support for the organizing of the *interahamwe* militias that carried out the 1994 genocide. Agencies must integrate explicit analyses of conflict, political impact, and human rights effects throughout planning, design, and implementation, including sensitivity to the latent tensions a project might activate. Finally, agencies must also look to history to understand and anticipate conflicts, rather than to static pictures of people's needs and relations.[30]

An important aspect of planning for peace building is remaining flexible enough to respond to situations that might allow for positive interventions in support of local-level reconciliation. In the Atar-Ayod-Kongor corridor in southern Sudan, local commanders were key in restoring a tenuous peace in an area racked by intercommunal and interfactional violence. OLS and its associated NGOs were also an important factor in facilitating this truce through their aid provision and constant engagement with the commanders on issues of humanitarian principle.

Such flexible interventions sometimes include small, in-kind support for local-level conflict-resolution conferences. For example, a number of agencies supported the Akobo Peace Conference in 1994, an attempt to reduce the intra-Nuer fighting that had increasingly plagued that region. The conflicting parties estimate that 1,300 people were killed and 75,000 cattle were raided. Chiefs led a forty-five-day reconciliation meeting based on customary law and traditional mediation approaches. After the conference, one agency lent a boat to Riek Machar, the main rebel commander in the area, to ply the Akobo and Sobat rivers in an effort to support the implementation of the peace agreement.[31]

Some agencies facilitated dialogue in Somaliland in the early 1990s by donating or lending radio equipment—including transmitters—to the warring parties. In Somalia, some agencies have provided support for various grassroots peace conferences, such as those in Boraama, Erigavo, Baidoa, and Kismayu and various failed efforts in Mogadishu. A separate evaluation is being conducted of these kinds of peace initiatives in Somalia, but as an initial conclusion, the study author—Ken Menkhaus—notes, "Well-meaning NGOs have sponsored local peace conferences that have excluded important groups, or yielded new regional coalitions at a third party's expense, leading to charges that the NGO had taken sides in the dispute."[32]

One skeptical agency representative noted that "perhaps these conferences would have gone ahead without us. Conferences are often held even without NGO funding, although funding is usually sought. In the end, our funding is quite marginal."[33] Another diplomat concurred: "They want our money, but they don't need our money."

The degree of relevance is not the only concern about agencies involvement in peace-building work. After attending a conference organized by Mary Anderson at Harvard University, Ken Menkhaus summarizes the skepticism:

> Participants . . . feared that NGO expertise in primary health care or agriculture does not qualify them to facilitate politically sensitive peace-building work. . . . Incautious NGOs have also at times been tricked into funding peace conferences that never materialized. Finally, when engaging in "direct peace-building," NGOs must explicitly identify local partners in peace-building. That act exposes local individuals to potentially dangerous risks, especially in situations where powerful constituencies oppose peace. Mistakes in such environments can easily get people killed, and mistakes in such environments are easy for outsiders to make.[34]

The conference participants concluded that agencies should avoid direct peace-building activities. If they do proceed, they should involve people with expertise and experience. They also pointed to an important opening for "indirect peace-building" activities such as the ones described earlier in this chapter. Sectoral activities that cross lines of conflict in the context of their humanitarian objective hold the most promise.

The conferees offered an example involving a primary school system in a zone of conflict that holds cross-line discussions among teachers about the location, staffing, and curriculum of the schools. The rationale is to build "a new educational constituency which transcends the ethnic conflict."[35] The key is in the cross-line nature of the planning process, which remains, however, in the context of programming—schools, health, agriculture, animal health—that is already planned or operational. Positive elements of this "indirect peace building" were identified by the conferees: It is viewed as nonpolitical when in the context of sectoral programming; it creates safe space for communities on both sides of the line to meet and deepen contacts and improve communication across these lines, channels that are critical when disputes or misunderstandings arise that might lead to the escalation of conflict; and it directly presents communities with evidence of the positive results of cooperation. This "indirect peace building," the conferees concluded, "may be the single most effective contribution that relief and development agencies can make to the cause of conflict resolution and prevention in their areas of operation."[36]

One sympathetic donor official, noting the difficulty of getting funding for peace-building initiatives, suggests couching the activities in a humanitarian principles context. Another UN agency country director notes that DHA may in principle be in favor of supporting reconciliation in the context of humanitarian rights.

Support Peace Building Capacity

Related to the earlier discussion of capacity building, emergency interventions can also support local peacemakers and constituencies by virtue of whom the agencies utilize as local partners. Rudy von Bernuth holds that local institution building that supports participatory democratic processes and pluralism is the most effective method to ensure peace.[37] Again, the division of labor must be recognized at the local level as well. Some forms of social organization are geared toward service provision; others, such as elders' councils, are appropriate for conflict resolution; still others make sense as profit-seeking ventures. Much agency frustration results from naively trying to force groups from the latter two categories into undertaking service provision. If a *woreda* council in Ethiopia, a chiefs' court in Sudan, or an elders' council in Somalia exists already and shows a disposition toward resolving conflict, that priority should be respected and, in some cases, supported.

Relief and development aid not preceded by or including the strengthening of domestic conflict-management systems can create and exacerbate conflicts, such as the cattle-rustling endemic to pastoral groups, whose development concerns conflict management as much as economic improvement. Similarly, aid to farmers can raise tensions when it seems to legitimate disputed occupancy. Adams and Bradbury recommend supporting community or government institutions that can resolve competing claims before distributing inputs.[38]

The most important element of sustainable reconciliation is to build and support peace constituencies. John Paul Lederach of Eastern Mennonite College describes this element as meaning that aid organizations must view local people not as recipients but as resources for citizen-based peacemaking.[39]

War can be a positive catalyst particularly vis-à-vis women and gender relations, as women's groups are often among the new civil organizations that arise to challenge conflict and promote peace and rights. Aid organizations can support this process and help women to consolidate their gains against pressures to retrench when war ends.[40]

Social capital can be defined as institutional arrangements—trust, norms of reciprocity and tolerance, and associational networks—that foster voluntary cooperation and civic engagement and correlate them with effective, responsive government, economic development, and public well-being.[41] Although some believe that social capital is rooted in long history, recent experience suggests that even long-antagonistic parties can quickly create bases for cooperative social problem-solving.[42] Agencies should be cognizant of the important role social capital may play in the managing and resolution of conflict.

Traditional social organizations are often the means by which local communities resolve conflicts. In Ethiopia, for example, Eddir, Equb, and Mehaber are the primary indigenous formal associations. Eddir is a welfare institution; Equb is a savings association; and Mehabir is a mechanism for communal responsibility.[43]

Local organizations are also beginning to form that are directly involved in peacemaking. For example, the Committee for Restarting Pastoral Initiatives in Butare, Rwanda, composed of one Tutsi priest and one Hutu intellectual, is receiving some support. They are convinced that reconciliation must start at the grassroots. They have a newsletter for public education purposes and are facilitating the return of refugees. More established organizations with regional perspectives also exist, most notably the Nairobi Peace Initiative, InterAfrica Group, and People for Peace in Africa.

Women's peace groups are being formed as well, including the Sudan Women's Voice for Peace, the Burundi Women's Association for Peace, and a number of Somali, Ethiopian, and Rwandan organizations. At the local level, in southern Sudan, Mogadishu, and Somaliland, women have often acted as emissaries across lines of battle, their safety guaranteed by intermarriage or by the acceptance of women's commercial and ambassadorial roles as nonmilitary and thus nonthreatening. Nevertheless, it is important to not be uncritically sanguine about the role of women in peacemaking; humanitarian organizations and other interveners may tend to mythologize the intentions and role of women, who often crave justice even if it means the continuation of war. Hugo Slim of Oxford Brookes University elaborates: "I think we need to be aware that a new fashion of women peacemaking projects is emerging in NGOs. These may be to the 1990s what women's crafts and basket weaving projects were to the 1980s, and be based on similarly simplistic assumptions and generalizations about women's roles in society. I am wary of this new wave of 'designer peace projects' for women."[44]

The marginalization of traditional authority in some locations has had profound consequences, including the severing of channels for transmitting basic values and a consequent increase in the raping and killing of women and children.[45] In the efforts of international agencies to build local capacity and enhance participation, questions need to be constantly asked about whether traditional authority structures are being undermined and—given their repressive nature in some places and their role in preserving the social fabric in other places—whether they should be. Agencies cannot choose *not* to address these issues in their quest for neutrality because most interventions have the potential to empower or disempower certain segments of the community based on the composition and structure of planning and delivery mechanisms. Constantly monitoring these effects should be a responsibility assumed by outside agencies. Keen and Wilson suggest that aid can enable democratic, peaceful elements in society to compete for the loyalty of young men at risk of being lured into violence in the absence other opportunities—for example, channeling aid through Somali elders.[46] Somalis have been thrown back on clan and subclan structures to meet basic needs, including security, and adapt a wealth of traditional mechanisms to resolve interclan killings and scarce resource conflicts.[47]

In relations with local authorities, certain questions should be debated within and among agencies. Does supporting civilian structures and humanitarian arms of authorities reduce military-dictated policies? Has engaging these structures on rights issues given space for civilian peace-building initiatives? Does this form of capacity building promote a public welfare ethic that might reduce conquest imperatives?

Since the Chukudum convention held by the SPLA in April 1994, there has been a tentative assignment of certain responsibilities in some locations to local civilian authorities. In some places, the chiefs have reasserted their authority; in others, civilian structures have a role in some decisions. SPLA leader John Garang notes that "the military didn't want to let go of power. It is still a struggle—commanders must not feel they are losing out, yet they must lose out."[48] In Ethiopia, *woreda*-level councils are to play an increasingly important role in local decisionmaking, just as clan councils and district councils already are in Somalia. The aforementioned questions need to be asked when approaching these forms of authority.

Humanitarian organizations such as ERA, REST, SRRA, and RASS have provided a formal structure for international agencies to address issues of public welfare and humanitarian principles, with the assumption that their concerns would be taken to the leaders of the respective political movements. An argument is advanced (hard to measure but a valid hypothesis for further research) by those associated with capacity building of these and other organizations that such engagement provides a moderating influence on the movements and promotes reciprocity between movements and local populations. Supporters of capacity building also claim that engaging the SRRA and RASS—and encouraging constant cooperation—has contributed to the cessation of hostilities between the SPLA and SSIA for much of 1994 and through the first half of 1995.

Conflict-management training can be a very useful tool in developing a capacity for peace building in emergency operations. "There is major room for workshops on negotiation skills," says a UN agency field manager. "Basic techniques need to be taught. Agencies often have very young people who are not skilled in negotiation." The Center for the Strategic Initiatives of Women (CSIW) (under the Fund for Peace umbrella) has held important workshops for women leaders from throughout the Horn. A Strategic Initiative on the Horn of Africa is being formed by CSIW staff to do training and support field-based conflict management and prevention at the community level.

ABuGiDa, an indigenous Ethiopian NGO, has held training sessions in conflict management in which community mobilizers and party members have participated. Also in Ethiopia, the Ad Hoc Committee for Peace and Development has held workshops in Harar, South Arssi, Wollaita, and Wollega at which a mixed group of elders and party officials met and discussed their differences.

In April 1994 the New Sudan Council of Churches trained local peace monitors in Kenya in interpositioning to strengthen cease-fires and peace agreements and ultimately to develop institutional capabilities to peacefully transform local conflicts.

The Rwandan Ministry of Higher Education conducted a seminar on tolerance in May 1995, broaching difficult issues a year after the genocide. "It provided an excellent opportunity to discuss serious issues," says an observer. "It gave the participants some space for reflection." Also in Rwanda, Africans for Humanitarian Action (AHA), an Ethiopian-run NGO, is working on capacity building in conflict management. AHA has conducted three workshops for government, civic groups, and agencies, again giving people a chance to talk openly about the genocide. The participants formed a contact group out of one of the sessions to follow up the discussions and pursue the topic of conflict resolution. Managing ethnic, cultural, and social differences was a major theme.[49] Again in Rwanda, CRS cosponsored with Kanya Rwanda (a Rwandan human rights group) a workshop called Establishing Confidence Between and Among Rwandans. As a follow-up, they brought Hizkias Assefa of the Nairobi Peace Initiative to facilitate a reconciliation workshop with government, human rights groups, and the Catholic church.[50]

In Burundi, the Catholic Bishops Conference initiated a series of

workshops focusing on mutual respect, tolerance, self-critical reflection, and forgiveness. The workshops have been offered in a variety
of locations to different groups. Ken Hackett of CRS notes, "Major
religious institutions in different societies are well placed with the
capacity through natural structures to minimize ethnic, economic,
racial, or religious divisions by reaching all levels of society." For
example, the Burundian bishops

> have called on civic and political leaders to attain higher standards
> of civic responsibility, self-critical awareness and egalitarian atti-
> tudes toward others. The politicians, the urban educated, the rural
> farmers and the children of all these groups are hearing this appeal
> spoken in their parishes and dioceses. It is hoped that this values-
> based approach is reaching the hearts of the Burundian people to
> promote unity and will act as a force to resist further genocide.[51]

Peace education programs are being explored by certain agencies, based in schools, communities, media, and religious institutions.
One agency official proclaimed that in Rwanda, "there must be a
massive education program to new ideas of inclusivity." Consequently, the Ministry of Higher Education in Rwanda is undertaking a
major initiative. One of the first steps is the training of mobilizers in
primary and secondary schools. There are plans to introduce peace
education into the school curriculum, stressing ways in which people
and communities have overcome past differences and reintegrated.
In Mogadishu, the Somali women's organization IIDA promotes
peace education in the context of a skills training program. In
Burundi, there is a children's game called *batissons la paix* (let's build
peace) that UNICEF uses with mixed groups of kids. The peace education program Search for Common Ground in Burundi is being
reviewed in mid-1996 and should uncover some important lessons.
    Regarding peace education, a UNICEF field manager points out,
"The promotion of tolerance and the acceptance of differences
through peace education is important." Pierce Gerety, former
UNICEF country director in Somalia, cautions,

> I'm concerned that some so-called peace education may be set
> up in a simplistic, shallow way that does not relate to how people
> really make decisions affecting their (or their community's) vital
> interests. Real peace education, to the extent that it is feasible, is a
> very long-term undertaking that involves changing the way indi-
> viduals, beginning as young children, learn to look at other people
> and to define themselves as members of a particular group in oppo-
> sition to others. It is a highly worthwhile enterprise, but it unfortu-
> nately does not offer an immediate solution to the conflicts that

have ripped these countries apart, conflicts that are based on manipulation of people's sense of insecurity, on leaders hungry for power
convincing followers who are just plain hungry that "if we don't
destroy our opponent they will destroy us." I think peace education
is something that has to be built carefully, brick by brick, on the
basis of an understanding of the human capacity for hatred and evil,
and of the genuine conflicts of interests between groups, not simply
appeals to good sentiments and human solidarity.

One place to begin is in removing the lessons of distrust and
hate that are contained in history lessons in many, if not most,
national curricula. It's amazing how easily children who have never
even met someone from a neighboring country or clan can assimi-
late lessons about the harm that "they" did, or may do, to "us."

Another good beginning is in learning through practice different methods of conflict resolution—talking things out or seeking
mediation rather than reaching for a weapon. But I have to recognize some of the peoples who are the most devoted to talking things
out until they reach consensus are also among the most inclined to
take up arms against their neighbors.

We should and must promote "peace education," but we must
recognize that to be effective it has to come in all sincerity from the
people directly concerned: It is clear from recent history that lessons
of harmony in school cannot by themselves overcome traditions of
prejudice passed on at home. It may well be a way to save [some]
future generations from the scourge of war, but it probably can't
provide an immediate solution to the conflicts that currently afflict
us.[52]

The most well-developed adult education program in the Greater
Horn that might address some of the above concerns is the
Development Education for Leadership Teams in Action (DELTA)
training pioneered in Kenya but now utilized worldwide, based on
the work of Brazilian educator Paulo Freire. The process engages a
community to solve problems jointly. Reflection and action processes
are designed so that communities examine societal cleavages and
pursue social change.[53]

The United Nations Educational, Scientific, and Cultural
Organization (UNESCO) and other agencies have introduced the
Culture of Peace program in Burundi. There is one peace educator,
one human rights promoter, one person who looks at the manner in
which local culture can promote peace, and one media strategist.
They have initiated colloquia and seminars for talking about peace
with students and other groups and have a plan to study cases of traditional reconciliation using the University of Burundi. Teachers and
students will collaborate with UNESCO.

Peace radio has been initiated in Somalia and Rwanda. From
Ethiopia, InterAfrica Group—on behalf of UNICEF—broadcasts a

peace program into Somalia on a daily basis. Radio is by far the most influential means of communication in Somalia, a highly oral society. Specific links are made on the peace radio programs among peace, protection of women and children, and religious traditions. A UNESCO Symposium on Somali Peace and Reconciliation urged more media programs presenting positive images of such components of peace building as traditional conciliation mechanisms and human rights rather than violence.[54]

UNHCR is doing radio broadcasts in Rwanda and the refugee camps in neighboring Zaire and Tanzania showing that people can return to Rwanda. UNICEF is collaborating with the Rwandan Ministry of Higher Education to produce a series of radio messages on cultural differences. In Burundi, an interview was broadcast with a returnee sitting next to people whom rumor had said were killed.

After the killing of the two presidents in April 1994, the Burundian government gave permission to the Bible Society of Rwanda to broadcast Christian appeals to the citizenry for peace in Burundi. The speaker of the parliament spoke of the need for calm and urged people not to take revenge. Similarly, UNITAF gave time on its radio station to traditional and Islamic leaders to resuscitate their authority.[55]

There are also video-based efforts at peace education, including the tailoring of peace programming for television. One of the summit meetings of Great Lakes presidents organized by the Carter Center brought about an agreement to videotape promises of safe return for the two million refugees from Rwanda and Burundi in neighboring countries. The leaders of five countries began taping appeals in mid-March 1996.

Enhancing Other Programming Strategies

Support Justice Systems

In every society, legal systems can contribute to reducing sources of violence and establishing the rule of law except when those systems are part of a security apparatus designed for repression rather than justice. International agencies (especially human rights groups whose usual mandate is only one of monitoring and reporting) should be open to opportunities that arise to build and support the capacity of legal systems that have the potential of reducing violence, even in the context of emergency programming.

Governmental justice systems are usually the terrain of bilateral democratization aid programs that fall under the development assistance category. For example, in Ethiopia under Mengistu Haile Mariam there was no independent judiciary, so it must be created from scratch. Also, particular aspects of the legal system can be isolated for specific assistance. In many chronic conflicts, land tenure is an igniting issue. In Ethiopia and Rwanda, this area should be singled out for capacity building, especially for the area of local tenure-dispute resolution.

But there are situations in which the judicial apparatus requires significant inputs in the emergency phase, such as postgenocide Rwanda and preexplosion Burundi. USAID was handcuffed by internal legal obstacles in its ability to aid the Rwandan justice system and by mid-1995 was still seeking a waiver in order to move forward with assistance. Donors with legal restrictions preventing the provision of assistance (relief and developmental) for justice systems should review and amend their response framework to allow for the aiding of justice systems, especially in countries emerging from complex emergencies. For example, the UN Special Rapporteur for Human Rights in Burundi recommended supporting the assistance of magistrates from other African nations in the reform and strengthening of judicial processes in Burundi.[56] Donors and operational agencies need the flexibility in the field to be able to support such initiatives if they become possible, such as in Rwanda, where an agency called Citizens Network is assisting in judicial training to build the capacity of the system.

Sufficient time must be given to a process of building or rebuilding justice systems. "The tendency is to want to build a large—and largely urban—'justice infrastructure' as opposed to taking sufficient time required to build a grassroots justice system from the bottom up," notes a donor agency official.

Furthermore, the success of the international tribunal in Rwanda will have a significant impact on any eventual peace process, as the party line in the Rwandan government remains "no reconciliation until justice." The *Commission de Triage,* which seeks to absolve persons wrongly accused of participating in the genocide, is failing to address even a small percentage of disputed cases and needs support so a balanced process can move forward.

Traditional courts at the local level are usually stabilizing influences within and between communities. In some parts of southern Sudan, a revival of culture is under way in which communities are solidifying and updating traditional law. This revival is a response to the breakdown of order and values that has accompanied the endless civil war, intensified by the intercommunal and interfactional fighting that has plagued the region since 1991.

In Nuer areas of Upper Nile, especially after the Akobo Peace Conference, the chiefs have been reasserting their authority in the area of customary law, with the support of some SSIM commanders. In Lotuko areas in Eastern Equatoria, community leaders are updating, monitoring, and enforcing customary law in the context of locally initiated processes of *emwara* (reconciliation). In Dinka areas of southern Bahr al-Ghazal, there is a reassertion of the authority of chiefs' courts in the context of the post–Chukudum Conference devolution of SPLA authority to civilian structures. (One executive chief in the area points out, "We are the opposite of the Nuer. We want to have broader discussion than just the chiefs. I don't want any one person making the law.") In the context of a fledgling grassroots peace process between Nuer and Dinka communities throughout early 1995, border chiefs reasserted their authority, based on tradition, history, and their role as witnesses and arbitrators. In Xande areas in Western Equatoria, a museum of culture has been established, and interest in traditional law has increased. In some of these areas, soldiers can now be taken to court when they commit civil offenses.

In times of economic stress, local courts can play a major role in conflict prevention. In the Waat area of Upper Nile in southern Sudan, traditional chiefs have convened "hunger courts" to enforce a more equitable distribution of milk cows throughout the community.[57]

Similarities among traditional legal systems in different areas provide a basis for cross-line harmonization of justice. "The Dinka, Nuer, and Shilluk have roughly the same customary laws," says one southern Sudanese commander. "This could minimize conflict,"[58] or at least provide the basis for broader dialogue. The Humanitarian Principles section of UNICEF in southern Sudan is studying and discussing indigenous notions of justice, partly to inform programming and partly to synthesize the complementarities between international law (particularly the Convention on the Rights of the Child) and Sudanese values.

The Sharia Courts proliferating in Somalia deserve mention. In many places they are arising in response to community demands for security. In Mogadishu North, Abgal religious leaders are funded by the community to enforce Sharia. Even after acknowledging this, Ahmed Mumin Warfa, a Somali peace activist, noted that in that place it is "a businessmen's vigilante effort."[59] Women's opinions are split regarding the courts. Some fear an erosion of rights, while others express satisfaction at the protection the courts afford them against violent acts such as rape, which had increased dramatically since the onset of the civil war.[60]

Support Demobilization

Demobilizing militia is usually conceived of in the postconflict context. Given the chronic nature of conflict in the Horn, demobilization should be couched in terms of the development of alternative livelihoods, that is, the creation of incentives to leave full-time soldier or militia status. The longer this issue of livelihoods is not addressed, the bigger the ticking time bomb gets as more and more young men are formed by the exclusive experience of fighting for a living.

Uganda, Ethiopia, and Eritrea have already undertaken demobilization programs that hold lessons for other countries. In Ethiopia, ex-soldiers received land and credit and were offered vocational training. Donor aid came rather late in the form of seeds, fertilizers, plastic tubing for coffee seedlings, and vehicles for administrative capacity.

In Somaliland, the Somali veterans' organization Soyaal addresses the needs of ex–militia members, as does the National Demobilization Commission. The latter was supported by UNDP with consultancy help from Zimbabwean veterans of demobilization, which helped to teach the importance of integrating demobilization programs into the wider social context. (An NGO called the Zimbabwe Project supports ex-fighters' projects.) Similarly, when the TPLF demobilized fighters, it held extensive and widespread discussions with the local communities into which the soldiers were moving back.[61]

Uganda's long experience in demobilization shows the value of providing low-interest loans to ex-fighters, given the fact that many microenterprises strangle from a lack of finance in their early stages. The NGO Ugandan Veterans Assistance Board (headed by two ex–ministers of defense and an academic) was not able to help provide credit, so the private sector, government, and donors had to fill the gaps.[62]

The SPLA has submitted proposals for the creation of farm cooperatives. The SPLA already has experience with farming, some of which includes fairly heinous practices of forced labor drawn from the surrounding communities, especially in Eastern Equatoria in the early 1990s. The SPLA now has a cooperative in Tambura (Western Equatoria), which has been assisted with farming inputs. Soldiers are farming and trading surplus at the CARE bush shop. "Before they were stealing from the agencies," says one observer. "Now they are trading with them." John Garang supports the idea, saying the SPLA "could produce as much as possible."[63] There are huge obstacles in terms of organization, discipline, experience, and cohesion, but the majority of SPLA soldiers, especially Dinka and Nuer, come from pastoral backgrounds.

In Somalia, UNOSOM's so-called 3-D division (Disarmament, Demobilization, and De-mining) produced nothing but excuses and high salaries for its expert employees and consultants. Superficial programs might do more harm than good. Research on armed Mogadishu youth gangs suggests that cash-for-guns disarmament programs only superficially address, and may exacerbate, the socioeconomic problem of militarized youth.[64]

In Somalia, monetization programs have generated substantial amounts of local currency used for rehabilitation initiatives. A strategic, participatory plan could be developed around these funds to directly and holistically address demobilization objectives, including the training, inputs, initial credit, and market development that sustainable initiatives require. Fisheries, livestock, agriculture, and trade are areas to explore. Port development is another area that holds much promise for sustainable employment. (Six thousand people were employed during UNOSOM's occupation, who in turn supported perhaps 30,000 family members.[65]) Food for work, on the other hand, is expensive make-work with no sustainability component. "The militia will laugh at food for work," claims an agency field official.

Adams and Bradbury note creative NGO demobilization support programs in Eritrea, Somaliland, and elsewhere (such as training ex-fighters as economic units—e.g., in brick-making—to exploit their teamwork skills) but note that such schemes can reach few people and cannot relieve governments of the major challenge of reintegrating soldiers and meeting their social and psychological as well as economic needs.[66]

Demobilization efforts in postwar economies such as those of Ethiopia—where new leaders inherit a "control regime" after significant capital flight, in the words of a Center for the Study of African Economies study—should aim to induce repatriation of capital to facilitate private investment.[67]

Collier notes the threat that massive demobilization—such as that of 400,000 Ethiopian soldiers in 1991–1992—threatens security through microinsecurity (fear of crime) and macroinsecurity (fear of government overthrow), noting that microinsecurity not only entails the immediate crime but inhibits investment and disrupts transactions.[68]

Comparing demobilized soldiers in 1992 Uganda and Ethiopia, Collier notes that the former were less well suited to demobilize because they were largely young, scantily educated, rural, guerrilla recruits during the war. In both cases the soldiers' years in the army had atrophied their connections to their home areas, and thus access to land, while allowing many to acquire dependents and thus need a substantial income. Guns were widely available.[69]

Transition policies for demobilized Ugandan and Ethiopian soldiers have largely been unnecessary and have failed. Collier describes thin financial and material aid to all demobilized soldiers with small, overly expensive job-creation schemes benefiting only a few and proving economically inviable. The schemes focused on construction labor, which requires skill in urban areas and is most efficient when using large numbers of unskilled local laborers—with their own housing and food—in rural areas rather than demobilized labor gangs.[70] Any training that does take place should be relevant to the private sector job market to which the trainee will be returning.

Integrate Psychosocial Programming

Addressing the specific needs of children is increasingly recognized as integral to any emergency response. Angela Raven-Roberts of UNICEF summarizes the plight of young people, calling them "the fodder for conflicts of the future: they have been marginalized, disenfranchised, thrown out of history, thrown out of culture, and thrown out of economics. [It is these people] who are going to be the perpetrators of new conflicts in the future."[71]

Providing psychosocial services is a critical component of a holistic response to complex emergencies. Magne Raundelen, the child psychologist who helped develop the psychosocial programs in Mozambique and Sudan, also undertook training sessions for Somali teachers. But the Somali training was short and had no follow-up. Psychosocial initiatives require a long-term commitment. In Mostar, Bosnia, a psychologist came every month to train teachers for a week at a time. "If you just bring in a consultant to raise the issues and don't follow up, you leave people open like wounds with no chance for healing," says one agency field representative.

Soon after the Rwandan genocide, USAID provided money for psychosocial programming. Children were being warehoused, and the trauma of what had preceded their arrival was being compounded by the horrible conditions of their new setting. A few agencies responded to these conditions in the camps and inside Rwanda, providing aid that included counseling services for children. SCF—US placed community youth workers in the centers in which the children were residing. In Kigali, local forms of social organization for children were supported, such as scouts, traditional dance groups, football teams, and church groups. Community discussions were held about the future of the children. "Culture is the only thing big enough to help," asserts the director of an agency. Africans for Humanitarian Action, an Ethiopian-based organization, also provides psychosocial trauma management, especially to Rwandese women. In addition, UNICEF has conducted seminars and training sessions in psychosocial trauma care.

The multidonor evaluation of the Rwandan emergency response critiques the overall efforts at psychosocial healing:

> Because neighbors, teachers, doctors and religious leaders took part in the carnage, essential trust in social institutions has been destroyed, replaced by pervasive fear, hostility and insecurity. The social upheaval has affected interpersonal and community interaction across ethnic, economic, generational and political lines. . . .
>
> Relatively little attention has been paid to the problem of psycho-social healing. Donor efforts have concentrated primarily on trauma counseling for children. . . . What few programs there have been for psycho-social healing have tended to overlook the needs of women. Also, the international community may be misapplying its experience with post–traumatic stress disorder. Missed opportunities in exploring indigenous concepts of mental health and methods of healing conceivably stem from initial lack of understanding of Rwandese society, psyche and culture, and the absence of adequate language skills, so vital to confidential communication.[72]

In Sudan, an estimated 20,000 children have been separated from their parents or guardians over the course of the civil war. Without the security of home or family, these children have been forced to fend for themselves, shifting frequently from one temporary camp to another as fighting raged in Sudan and in neighboring Ethiopia, where many sought refuge. Since 1988, most of these unaccompanied children have trekked hundreds of miles before settling in isolated communities.[73]

The unaccompanied minors are virtually all boys between eight and sixteen years old. In 1988, after the war in the south escalated, thousands walked toward Ethiopia from western Upper Nile and Bahr al-Ghazal, hundreds of kilometers away. Most lived in the Sudanese refugee camps at Itang, Panyido, and Dima in western Ethiopia until they were forced to flee back to Sudan with the fall of the Mengistu regime in Ethiopia in mid-1991. Psychosocial services are a major part of the response to the needs of these children by UNICEF and a few NGOs.

6

Carrot-and-Stick Humanitarianism: Aid Conditions for Peace

Aid conditionalities for development and security assistance are well-established tools of foreign policy, but humanitarian assistance to areas of the world not of vital strategic importance has been largely exempt from such overt conditions. Nevertheless, many agencies continuously experiment with conditionalities on the ground, often operating outside any agreed-upon framework.

There are many issues that might be addressed by such conditionality, such as human rights, reciprocity, humanitarian principles, seriousness at the negotiating table, security of aid personnel, and costs. Some of these issues will be explored below.

As noted earlier, humanitarian assistance is usually by far the largest input into a war-torn society from external donors. Food and medical aid are particularly valuable to combatants, and they hold tremendous potential leverage for conditionalities based on humanitarian principle and reconciliation.

Should aid be cut off in certain situations? "There is a growing consideration of introducing conditionalities on humanitarian aid linked to agreements on adherence to agreed-upon principles," observes Philip O'Brien of UNICEF. "Aid should only be suspended, though, within the framework of an agreement with authorities."[1] The decision to stop assistance is often traumatic for an agency. The loss of access, information, and witness is usually judged to be so grave that most agencies will not completely withdraw from an area unless the emergency is completely over or the security situation is untenable. The flip side of this is that if an agency is not doing anything positive by its presence, is it de facto condoning the situation if it is not speaking out?

In the context of Sudan, for example, questions about the use of aid to underwrite Khartoum's war efforts remain unanswered. To what extent is the international community assuming the public welfare responsibilities of the Sudanese government, thereby freeing resources for the war? Are aid flights from Khartoum to the south supplying provisions to government garrisons rather than civilians in need? Is money spent in the pursuit of aid projects providing the government with a source of hard currency used to prosecute the war, and are donated food stocks in the north freeing Sudanese grain production for export? If donors cannot independently investigate and resolve these issues satisfactorily, then their entire aid program to the north should be reconsidered. Yet any cutoff or suspension should be conditioned scrupulously on consistent abuse of access, accountability, and reciprocity, and the same principles should be applied to aid to the south.[2]

Decisions about withdrawal should be coordinated among agencies. For example, MSF withdrew from Goma and raised public awareness of a critical political problem. Agencies that stayed behind continue to provide needed humanitarian inputs, maintain a semblance of regional stability, and (in some cases) quietly provide information to human rights organizations about the situation in the camps. If many donor countries continue to shy away from political engagement in this thorny affair, at the least they could help coordinate this division of responsibility between public condemnation and quiet assistance.

Other principles than agency security are rarely invoked for a cessation of humanitarian assistance. Some of these issues are touched on later. Also, geopolitics continues to play a role in humanitarian response, as some donors are reluctant to provide humanitarian assistance to government-held areas of Sudan not just because of the continuous violation of numerous humanitarian principles but also because of the regional destabilization agenda and the internal human rights violations of the National Islamic Front–controlled government.

One of the most critical determinants of whether and how to invoke conditions is to canvass the target population's viewpoints on the issue to the maximum extent possible. What do the people think? Should the agencies go public about certain abuses and withdraw or be kicked out? Should the agencies continue with their limited inputs in silence?[3]

Making Aid Conditional on Humanitarian Principles

In highly insecure situations, donors are usually dependent on the degree of risk NGOs are prepared to accept to reach an affected population. Agencies usually carry out their own subjective cost-benefit analyses regarding whether they will or can respond to a particular crisis. There is increasing interest in looking at humanitarian principles as a guide for response. In Chapter 3, I examined the Code of Conduct in Somalia and the ground rules in Sudan as two examples of principles in action. Below are some cases in which aid was cut off for reasons related to humanitarian principle.

In Kenya, the Somali refugee camps in Mandera, El Wak, and Liboi were closed by UNHCR despite the opposition of the camp population. Costs were enormous, an asylum option remained, and the security situation had stabilized inside Somalia to allow repatriation (some argue that the situation inside most of Somalia was safer than that inside the camps).

When SCF—UK pulled out of Mogadishu completely, other agencies were sympathetic. SCF had experienced death threats to staff from the outside and by other staff members (Habr Gedir against Bantu), kidnapping, and exorbitant costs measured against very small benefits. The agency pulled out of Belet Weyne in August 1995 when the local health authority with which SCF had been working told agency officials that they weren't doing any good given the political infighting extant in that town.

Not every situation is so clear. In a case of mutual culpability, a dispute between WFP and General Sayid Hersi "Morgan" in Kismayu, Somalia, led to a cutoff of all nonemergency assistance to that city. This cutoff gradually created a precarious nutritional situation in the feeding centers and hospital in Kismayu. One agency official decries this decision: "Does any agency have the right to deny assistance to people who can't speak for themselves in situations of crisis?" In looting situations, "seeds shouldn't be stopped if some authority loots 10 percent of them."

On the Zairian border, Ijwi Island camp contains 40,000 Rwandan refugees. It is a known launching pad for infiltration of the former government military and *interahamwe*. Agencies planned to eventually cease aid to the island and either move the population farther into Zaire or lure the people back to Rwanda. The eventual goal is to have no camp within fifty miles of the Rwanda-Zaire border.

Some agencies (such as International Rescue Committee, CARE—Canada, and MSF—France) and donors have withdrawn from the camps in Zaire altogether, claiming that their aid was reinforcing the power structures that were responsible for the genocide and that the genocide organizers were holding the refugees hostage, which made work in the camps incompatible with humanitarian principles.[4] Others worry about the ramifications of such action if done collectively: "Total withdrawal would provoke chaos, looting, and violence," claims an agency regional head, noting that cutting off water alone would create epidemics within days. "It is a myth that material conditions influence repatriation decisions. Plus, there is a role for aid in keeping the lid on an explosive situation. This becomes a problem when keeping the lid on becomes the objective rather than addressing the political roots."

(Though international aid community criticism and real and threatened withdrawals led the Rwandan government-in-exile to conduct a concerted effort to improve the public image of the camps—by holding elections, reorganizing security, sending uniformed soldiers away from the camps, ending open militia training, and fostering civic organizations—the changes were largely "cosmetic."[5])

In November 1994, ECHO decided to stop all funding for NGOs serving the internally displaced camps within Rwanda, hoping to create a push factor to move people back to their home areas. The results of the experiment were unclear because some agencies with independent sources of funding remained in the camps, viewing their continued assistance as a humanitarian imperative.

As well as the outright cessation of aid, sequential conditions regarding the security and independence of aid assets and personnel are often set for continuing assistance. In response to the looting of cars in Eastern Equatoria, SCF—UK (boreholes), WFP (food), Sudan Medical Care (medicine), and Diocese of Torit (animal health) teamed together to make safety on the roads a condition of continuing to provide inputs. The conditionality was based on the principle of unfettered, secure access. The SPLA was concerned enough about the plight of the Bor Dinka in the displaced camps that it ensured the cessation of raiding of vehicles. The new consortium of some of the NGOs operating in southern Sudan is developing a unified response to particularly egregious abuses by all parties to the conflict and looking at conditionalities related to independent access, monitoring, and assessment.

Making Aid Conditional on Progress in Conflict Resolution

Continuous cycles of conflict produce impatience and frustration on the part of donors and agencies, as they repeatedly place Band-Aids over the wounds opened and reopened by the fighting. Questions are being asked about whether those responding ought to be more assertive in addressing such conflicts and whether there may be situations when humanitarian assistance should be conditioned on progress toward peace, or at least cessation of hostilities at the local or national level. In any case, any conditionality in this arena requires extreme sophistication of understanding of the local context in which one is operating.

SEOC emulated the "tough love" approach initiated by the ecumenical agencies involved in the Ethiopian and Eritrean cross-border relief operation. Lutheran World Relief noted in 1989 that extended, expensive relief could prolong conflict by enabling warring parties to evade their responsibility to civilians and urged agencies to seriously consider withholding aid if peace efforts failed; the ecumenical agencies maintained this stance throughout the war. Lutheran World Relief's executive director declared in 1991 that the time had come to begin to "question the effectiveness of paying endless millions for humanitarian aid which may only be exacerbating and prolonging the conflict . . . [and maybe] for humanitarian assistance to be tied to some strings." He went so far as to disavow the useless adage that food should not be used as a political weapon and urged its positive use to force peace negotiations.[6] In Sudan, Lutheran World Federation officials similarly worried that the expensive Juba airlift could prolong the war and, in forming SEOC, threatened to withdraw aid unless the warring parties permitted road transport.[7]

A Sudanese employee of an NGO believes that conditionality might facilitate reconciliation between the Dinka and Nuer—and more broadly the SPLA and SSIA: "Giving aid unconditionally emboldens the warmakers." But this course of action, he warns, can have other side effects: "If we cut aid, we will weaken the people even more in their efforts to defend themselves against the government offensives."

Earlier chapters of this book have examined using conditions on animal health services as an entry point to address constant cattle raiding. "Maybe we should go in and ask the community what they will guarantee in the way of a good operating environment," suggests one war-zone veterinarian. "Let them determine the ground rules, the sanctions. Then if a raid happens and they have promised not to raid, maybe we should withhold services from the raiders."[8] Or even more proactively, proffers Philip O'Brien of OLS, "we could build into the program that the price of cattle vaccination is to not raid."[9]

Once an acute emergency phase is over, the opportunities to introduce these kinds of conditions increase. "The emergency mandate is to save the drowning person," says one donor official. "When the person is out of the water, we need to get tougher politically. We shouldn't go beyond the basics until there is peace." Willet Weeks cautions, "Downgrading to emergency Band-Aid inputs is very dangerous. We have to focus on rehabilitation."[10] Yet another nuance is expressed by Geoffry Loane: "We cannot become part of a political decisionmaking process. The independence of aid must be retained. Political decisions must be separated from basic rights to aid. Aid workers lose their security if identified with the politics of the international community."[11] In a play on the food-as-a-weapon motif, Kevin Ashley concurs: "You can't use relief as a weapon,"[12] meaning that emergency aid should not be used as a tool of peacemakers. The difficulty in achieving consensus on this issue is summed up by Rowland Roome of CARE—Rwanda: "Too often the people who don't care and are not affected are the rulers. The people would suffer. But there should be political conditions on moving up the [aid] continuum."[13]

Conditioning aid on progress on peace agreements is very tricky. "Having these kinds of requirements would give abusive authorities a silver platter for stopping aid," says a former agency regional manager.[14] In Sudan, for example, cutting off international aid to the two main warring parties—the government and the SPLA—would hurt the latter disproportionately. But in Angola, when Jonas Savimbi of the National Union for the Total Independence of Angola (UNITA) walked away from the peace agreement after the 1992 elections, aid was cut significantly by certain donors.

Positive conditionality is utilized more frequently, such as the SACB's condition for rehabilitation only in secure areas. "If you do X, we'll give you Y," suggests a UN regional official, noting that land tenure and arrest procedures should be items for consideration in Rwanda. A question underlying positive conditionality is whether the pattern of incentives can be changed enough to change the behavior of an authority. Can an interest be created in peace? Can war prosecutors benefit from peace under certain conditions? Should carrots be offered in the emergency phase? One cautionary note is sounded by a donor official: "Humanitarians make lousy politicians. They don't use their tremendous potential to influence events."

The issue of "reverse conditionality" must also be more widely debated and discussed. Gayle Smith of USAID cautions, "Great emphasis is given to holding warring parties accountable, but it is rarely acknowledged that *we* are not accountable and we often exacerbate the conflict. Should the conditionality all go one way?" Clearly not. The push for improved standards and codes of conduct must be combined with a serious search for enhanced accountability on the part of those responding to crises.

Concluding Thoughts

In most complex political emergencies, humanitarian aid is the most important avenue of contact among the international community, the conflicting parties, and civilians in the war zones. Ignoring the wider impacts and potential of humanitarian aid removes one of the most important policy instruments for preventing the escalation of conflict and promoting long-term peace building.

The compartmentalization of relief and development hinders the flexibility needed in the field to address some of the fundamental issues that might prevent conflict or its exacerbation by aid. Aside from the importance of understanding the interconnectedness of relief and development, much more attention needs to be given to what the objectives of development itself actually are. It is clear that in the current global context of Africa's marginalization, and the damaging results dominant models of development have had in Africa, profound rethinking is required of the very process of development itself for a region as fragile as the Greater Horn. Furthermore, Ethiopia's vision of development may differ greatly over time from Tanzania's, and development in the chronic conflict in southern Sudan may take a radically different form than that in Somaliland. The search for more appropriate African alternatives requires flexibility, experimentation, and openness on the part of donors and operational agencies.

In this search for alternative development strategies, a broad cross-section of the population throughout the region should be consulted and involved. Facilitating consultations at the local level throughout the Greater Horn on basic questions of development, human and civil rights, the nature of participatory political processes, and the direction of particular peace processes[1] would provide a valuable ingredient for a more stable and just regional order. Certain subregional organizations—InterAfrica Group, Nairobi Peace Initiative, All Africa Conference of Churches, IGAD—would be appropriate co-conveners on specific issues. In some cases this process is already happening, as with InterAfrica Group's consultations on a variety of specific issues such as the Ethiopian constitution,

143

women's role in politics, and humanitarian intervention in the Horn.

As addressed in Chapter 6, aid conditions must be rethought as well. Although development aid is often targeted for termination as part of a set of conditionalities, it is clear from the discussion in Chapter 2 that traditionally defined relief items (emergency food and medicine, primarily) are usually of greater strategic value than more developmentally oriented aid, which often has no military value whatsoever. More constructive use of positive conditionalities should be considered, particularly in the context of growing reliance by agencies in the field on codes of conduct and ground rules. Rewarding positive behavior by authorities toward their citizenry should be as integral to conditionality as circumventing or withdrawing aid from rights-abusing authorities.

Whether attempting to minimize the conflict-producing externalities of aid or to proactively contribute to peace building, the fundamental principle of supporting community structures and initiatives applies. In the former, building internal accountability is the key to reducing diversion and other inadvertent contributions to warring factions. In the latter, supporting local constituencies for peace and rebuilding social institutions are critical in laying the foundations for reduced violent conflict. The self-perception of the role of many NGOs is undergoing transformation, as the comment of Ken Hackett of CRS symbolizes: "Increasingly, the role of most international NGOs is to strengthen institutions within civil society which act as buffers and offer possibilities for dialogue to address structural, cultural and political tensions."[2] A major challenge for external interveners is to build on existing traditions of social organization, not externally conceived models such as local replicas of international NGOs. There is a danger of creating a context in which local groups' need to access funding warps organizational evolution and distances civil society leaders from their indigenous constituencies.[3]

Many analysts and field operators have noted that, given the increasing complexities faced by those responding to emergencies, a new type of politically astute humanitarian worker is needed. More training for the complex environments that must be faced should be a priority. Without a renewed commitment to relevant personnel and preparation, improvements in emergency response will be painstakingly slow.

Finally, there is really no substitute for improving the quality of the basics such as planning, assessing, monitoring, and evaluating. The devil is in the details, and part of the response to this increasingly complex reality may need to include less reliance on quantity of output and more on quality of input. Slowly changing the benchmarks of "success"—and educating the wider public about the importance of these changes—is critical.

Humanitarian aid will continue to be utilized as an instrument of war and will continue to fuel conflict. It is incumbent upon those providing aid to minimize this phenomenon and to consciously and strategically enhance aid's role in the peace-building process.

Notes

Chapter 1

1. Larry Minear and Thomas G. Weiss, *Humanitarian Action in Times of War* (Boulder, Colo.: Lynne Rienner Publishers, 1993).

2. Interview, Kabiru Kinyanjui, August 18, 1995.

3. Interview, Vincent Coultan, July 26, 1995.

4. John Borton, "Humanitarian Aid and Effects," in John Eriksson, *The International Response to Conflict and Genocide*, Synthesis Report, March 1996, p. 32. Contact Overseas Development Institute, Regent's College, London NW14NS.

5. David Rieff, "The Humanitarian Trap," *World Policy Journal*, Winter 1995/1996, p. 5.

6. Nicholas Stockton, "The Great Lakes and the Humanitarian Contract Culture," mimeo, October 1994.

7. Tanya Boudreau, remarks at a conference on food security in the Greater Horn sponsored by Save the Children Fund—US and InterAfrica Group, Addis Ababa, October 24, 1995.

8. D. Keen and K. Wilson, "Engaging with Violence: A Reassessment of Relief in Wartime," in J. Macrae and A. Zwi, eds., *War and Hunger: Rethinking International Responses to Complex Emergencies* (London: Zed, 1994), p. 209.

9. Emily MacFarquhar, Robert Rotberg, and Martha Chen, "NGOs, Early Warning, and Preventive Diplomacy," a report of a World Peace Foundation conference, 1995, p. 14.

10. The Ted Turner example was raised by Neta Crawford of Brown University at a conference on sovereignty and intervention in complex emergencies, Harvard University School of Population and Development Studies, April 1, 1996.

11. Stein Villumstad, "The Ecumenical Network and Complex Emergencies: Policy Challenges and Operational Options," mimeo, September 1995, p. 10.

12. Joelle Tanguy, remarks at a conference on sovereignty and intervention in complex emergencies, Harvard University School of Population and Development Studies, April 1, 1996.

13. Personal communication, Kathi Austin, January 24, 1996.

14. Personal correspondence, Ken Menkhaus, December 21, 1995.

15. This law was best described to me by Bengt Herring of the Swedish International Development Agency during discussions in southern Sudan in July 1993.

16. Interview, Willet Weeks, July 28, 1995.

17. Interview, Vincent Coultan, July 26, 1995.

18. Gordon Wagner, "Project Proposal: Humanitarian Institutional Exchanges in the Horn of Africa Between Ethiopia, Eritrea and Southern Sudan," p. 3.

19. Quoted in Rieff, p. 8.

20. Personal communication, Kathi Austin, January 24, 1996.

21. Interview, Ted Chaiban, June 20, 1995.

22. Interview, Vincent Coultan, July 26, 1995.

23. Interview, Geoffry Loane, August 17, 1995.

24. M. Duffield, J. Ryle, S. Jaspers, and H. Young, *SEOC Review,* 1995, p. 232.

25. Mark Duffield, discussion paper for Aid Under Fire conference, Wilton Park, London, April 1995, pp. 2–3 and 14.

26. Interview, Philip O'Brien, June 28, 1995.

27. Interview, Rowland Roome, August 7, 1995.

28. Mark Bradbury, "Aid Under Fire: Redefining Relief and Development Aid in Unstable Situations," Paper No. 104, Aid Under Fire conference, Wilton Park, London, April 1995, p. 19.

29. Personal communication, Kathi Austin, January 24, 1996.

30. Rieff, pp. 4–5.

31. Duffield, discussion paper, pp. 2–3 and 14.

32. Borton, p. 31.

33. John Eriksson, editor, *The International Response to Conflict and Genocide: Lessons from the Rwandan Experience* (Copenhagen: Standberg Grafisk, 1996).

Chapter 2

1. Gayle Smith, "On Studying War: Relief Operations and Military Strategy," mimeo, February 1993, p. 3.

2. D. Keen, "The Functions of Famine in Southwestern Sudan: Implications for Relief," in Macrae and Zwi, eds., *War and Hunger,* p. 121.

3. Cited in Stephen Buckley, "Aid Groups Snared in African Violence," *Washington Post,* January 23, 1996, p. A9.

4. Villumstad, p. 3.

5. J. Macrae and A. Zwi, "War and Hunger," in J. Macrae and A. Zwi, eds. *War and Hunger,* p. 301.

6. Ibid., p. 303.

7. Quoted in Buckley, p. A9.

8. Médecins sans Frontières (MSF), "Deadlock in the Rwandan Refugee Crisis: Virtual Standstill on Repatriation," agency mimeo June 1995, pp. 8–9.

9. Macrae and Zwi, 1994. "War and Hunger."

10. Interview, Kevin Ashley, June 16, 1995.

11. For classic case studies of this phenomenon, see Jemera Rone and John Prendergast, *Civilian Devastation: Human Rights Abuses by All Parties in the War in Sudan* (New York: Human Rights Watch, 1994).

12. Personal communication, Kathi Austin, January 24, 1996.

13. Interview, Andrew Natsios, September 25, 1995.

14. Interview, John Garang, June 28, 1995.

15. Keen and Wilson, "Engaging with Violence," pp. 212–213.

16. African Rights, "Imposing Empowerment," Discussion Paper No. 7, December 1995, p. 6.

17. Gordon Wagner, unpublished USAID trip report, February 1993, p. 5.

18. "News from Africa Watch," April 15, 1993, p. 8.

19. Interviews with Catholic Relief Services and World Vision officials in Torit and Nairobi, November 18–22, 1991.

20. Andrew Natsios, "Humanitarian Relief Interventions in Somalia: The Economics of Chaos," paper delivered at Princeton University conference, March 16, 1995, p. 5.

21. Alex de Waal, "Dangerous Precedents? Famine Relief in Somalia 1991–93," in Macrae and Zwi, eds., *War and Hunger*, p. 146.

22. MSF, p. 9.

23. Interview, Willet Weeks, July 28, 1995.

24. Interview, Andrew Natsios, September 25, 1995.

25. Mark Duffield, "The Political Economy of Internal War: Asset Transfer, Complex Emergencies and International Aid," in Macrae and Zwi, eds., *War and Hunger*, p. 60–61.

26. De Waal, "Dangerous Precedents?" pp. 146–147.

27. Personal communication, Kathi Austin, January 24, 1996.

28. Mark Adams and Mark Bradbury, "Conflict and Development: Background Paper for UNICEF/NGO Workshop," New York, April 27, 1995, p. 38.

29. David Tardif-Douglin and Krishna Kumar, "Rebuilding Post-Genocide Rwanda," in Eriksson, ed., *International Response*, p. 35.

30. Ken Menkhaus reminded me of the latter rationale in a personal correspondence, December 21, 1995.

31. Interview, Ahmed Mumin Warfa, July 1, 1995.

32. Personal communication, Kathi Austin, January 24, 1996.

33. Adams and Bradbury, p. 45.

34. Mary Anderson, "International Assistance and Conflict: An Exploration of Negative Impacts," mimeo, 1994, pp. 12–13.

35. Personal communication, Kathi Austin, January 24, 1996.

36. Macrae and Zwi, "War and Hunger," p. 27, citing Keen and Wilson, pp. 209–221.

37. Interview, Geoffry Loane, August 17, 1995.

38. Personal correspondence, Ken Menkhaus, December 21, 1995.

39. Interview, Vincent Coultan, July 26, 1995.

40. Adams and Bradbury, pp. 34–35.

41. Interview, Vincent Coultan, July 26, 1995.

42. Interview, Kevin Ashley, June 24, 1995.

43. *SEOC Review*, M. Duffield, J. Ryle, S. Jaspers, and H. Young, 1995, p. 178.

44. Ibid., p. 176.

45. Rieff, p. 9.

46. Africa Watch, *Evil Days* (New York: Human Rights Watch, 1990).

47. Mark Duffield and John Prendergast, *Without Troops and Tanks: Humanitarian Intervention in Ethiopia and Eritrea* (Trenton, N.J.: Red Sea Press, 1994).

48. MSF, p. 39.

49. Ibid., p. 7.

50. Personal correspondence, Ken Menkhaus, December 21, 1995.
51. Interview, Vincent Coultan, July 26, 1995.
52. Interview, Heywood Hadfield, July 10, 1995.
53. Personal communication, Gayle Smith, January 10, 1996.

Chapter 3

1. Interview, Abdi Aden Ali, July 1, 1995.
2. Alex de Waal, "Famine Mortality: A Case Study of Darfur, Sudan, 1984–85," *Population Studies* 43, 1989, pp. 5–24.
3. I first heard this term from Mary Anderson.
4. Interview, Pierce Gerety, July 2, 1995.
5. See, for example, Minear and Weiss, *Humanitarian Action in Times of War.*
6. Iain Levine, personal communication to Colin Scott and John Prendergast, November 14, 1995.
7. Iain Levine, "Report on Workshop on Humanitarian Principles for Sudanese NGOs," mimeo, April 1995, p. 8.
8. K. Menkhaus, "Conflict, Peace-building, and International Aid: The State of the Art," mimeo (1995), p. 2.
9. Macrae and Zwi, "War and Hunger," pp. 28–29.
10. Interview, Andrew Natsios, September 25, 1995.
11. Quoted in David Smock, "Humanitarian Assistance and Conflict in Africa," *Peaceworks,* U.S. Institute of Peace, 1996, p. 13.
12. Interview, Willet Weeks, July 28, 1995.
13. Mark Duffield and John Prendergast, "Sovereignty and Intervention After the Cold War," *Middle East Report,* March–June 1994, p. 15.
14. Minear and Weiss, *Humanitarian Action in Times of War,* p. 23.
15. Villumstad, p. 8.
16. Interview, Heywood Hadfield, July 10, 1995.
17. Interview, Geoffry Loane, August 17, 1995.
18. Bradbury, "Aid Under Fire"; and African Rights, "Humanitarianism Unbound?" Discussion Paper No. 5, 1994.
19. Quoted in Smock, p. 13.
20. Oxfam—UK/Ireland, "Community Managed Distribution; Oxfam—UK/I's Experience from East Africa," mimeo, 1994, p. 4.
21. African Rights, "Imposing Empowerment," p. 50.
22. International Federation of Red Cross Societies, *World Disasters Report,* Netherlands, 1994.
23. Larry Minear and Thomas G. Weiss, *Mercy Under Fire: War and the Global Humanitarian Community* (Boulder, Colo.: Westview 1995), p. 209.
24. Interview, Geoffry Loane, August 17, 1995.
25. Interview, Rowland Roome, August 7, 1995.
26. Interview, Vincent Coultan, July 26, 1995.
27. Interview, Helge Rohn, August 17, 1995.
28. Interview, Kevin Ashley, June 24, 1995.
29. Interview, Geoffry Loane, August 17, 1995.
30. Interview, John Ryle, August 25, 1995.
31. UN Department of Humanitarian Affairs (DHA), "Protection of

Humanitarian Mandates in Conflict Situations," mimeo, April 13, 1994, p. 4.

32. *SEOC Review,* M. Duffield, J. Ryle, S. Jaspers, and H. Young, 1995, p. 193.

33. Ibid., p. 221.

34. Bradbury, "Aid Under Fire," p. 32.

35. For further discussion, see Eriksson, ed., *International Response,* pp. 59–60.

36. Interview, Philip Winter, July 1, 1995.

37. Interview, Iain Levine, August 20, 1995.

38. Interview, Tim Leyland, July 5, 1995.

39. Interview, Kevin Ashley, June 24, 1995.

40. Interview, Philip Winter, July 1, 1995.

41. African Rights, "Imposing Empowerment," p. 19.

42. *FEWS Bulletin,* January 26, 1996, p. 2.

43. African Rights, "Imposing Empowerment," p. 21.

Chapter 4

1. Macrae and Zwi, "War and Hunger," p. 24.

2. Quoted in Smock, pp. 4–5.

3. Keen and Wilson, p. 209.

4. Jeff Drumtra, briefing, October 8, 1995.

5. Macrae and Zwi, "War and Hunger," p. 24.

6. Interview, Helge Rohn, August 17, 1995.

7. AID/BHR/OFDA, "Guidelines for Foreign Disaster Assistance," September 1, 1994.

8. Macrae and Zwi, 1994, p. 316.

9. Interview, Willet Weeks, July 28, 1995.

10. Ioan Lewis, remarks in Royal Anthropological Institute International NGOs and Complex Political Emergencies: Perspectives from Anthropology conference report, January 1995, p. 17.

11. Quoted in Smock, p. 5.

12. Borton, p. 27.

13. Interview, Walid Musa, July 10, 1995.

14. John Ryle and David Keen, prospectus for The Fate of Information in the Disaster Zone conference, September 27, 1995.

15. Personal communication, Kathi Austin, January 24, 1996.

16. H. Young and S. Jaspars, *Nutrition Matters—People, Food, and Famine* (London: Intermediate Technology Publications, 1995), p. 133.

17. Boudreau, Save the Children Fund—US and InterAfrica Group conference, October 24, 1995.

18. *SEOC Review,* M. Duffield, J. Ryle, S. Jaspers, and H. Young, 1995, pp. 125–127.

19. Interview, Kevin Ashley, June 24, 1995.

20. Interview, Tim Leyland, July 5, 1995

21. Alex de Waal, "A Reassessment of Entitlement Theory in the Light of Recent Famines in Africa," *Development and Change* 21, 1990, p. 469.

22. Interview, Vincent Coultan, July 26, 1995.

23. *SEOC Review,* M. Duffield, J. Ryle, S. Jaspers, and H. Young, 1995, p. 185.

24. Derived from my observations in the field as well as a personal communication from Ted Chaiban, January 4, 1996.

25. Interview, Andrew Natsios, September 25, 1995.

26. *SEOC Review,* M. Duffield, J. Ryle, S. Jaspers, and H. Young, 1995, p. 132.

27. Interview, Matt Bryden, July 2, 1995.

28. John Prendergast, "Helping or Hurting? Humanitarian Intervention in the Horn," Center of Concern Discussion Paper, 1995.

29. Villumstad, p. 5.

30. Minear and Weiss, *Mercy Under Fire,* p. 114.

31. *SEOC Review,* M. Duffield, J. Ryle, S. Jaspers, and H. Young, 1995, p. 240.

32. DHA, p. 4.

33. Adams and Bradbury, pp. 33–34.

34. John Prendergast, "The Gun Talks Louder Than the Voice: Somalia's Continuing Cycles of Violence," Center of Concern Discussion Paper, 1994.

35. Interview, Vincent Coultan, July 26, 1995.

36. Borton, p. 31.

37. MSF, pp. 14–15.

38. Personal communication, Kathi Austin, January 24, 1996.

39. Interview, David Neff, July 7, 1995.

40. Interview, Ali Salad Hassan, July 16, 1995.

41. Interview, Willet Weeks, July 28, 1995.

42. AICF survey data, May 1995.

43. *FEWS Bulletin,* January 26, 1996, p. 2.

44. Villumstad, p. 5.

45. Duffield and Prendergast, *Without Troops and Tanks.*

46. Interview, Matt Bryden, July 2, 1995.

47. Interview, Vincent Coultan, July 26, 1995.

48. Interview, Rowland Roome, August 7, 1995.

49. Interview, Matt Bryden, July 2, 1995.

50. Barbara Hendrie, "Cross-Border Operations in Eritrea and Tigray," *Disasters,* 1990 13 (4), pp. 351–60.

51. Interview, Willet Weeks, July 28, 1995.

52. Natsios, "Humanitarian Relief Interventions in Somalia," p. 10.

53. *SEOC Review,* M. Duffield, J. Ryle, S. Jaspers, and H. Young, 1995, p. 139.

54. *SEOC Review,* M. Duffield, J. Ryle, S. Jaspers, and H. Young, 1995, p. 101, citing similar observation in Mozambican and Liberian conflicts in Reginald Green, *Food and Famine,* Institute for Development Studies, mimeo, 1992.

55. Interview, Geoffry Loane, August 17, 1995.

56. Interview, Vincent Coultan, July 26, 1995.

57. John Sommer, *Hope Restored? Humanitarian Aid in Somalia, 1990–94* (Washington, D.C.: Refugee Policy Group, 1994).

58. Interview, Jean Martinique, July 9, 1995.

59. Personal communication, Kathi Austin, January 24, 1996.

60. Interview, Geoffry Loane, August 17, 1995.

61. Interview, Vincent Coultan, July 26, 1995.

62. *SEOC Review*, 1995, p. 142.

63. Oxfam—UK/Ireland, pp. 4–5.

64. Interview, Geoffry Loane, August 17, 1995.

65. Eriksson, ed., *International Response*, p. 63.

66. Interview, Willet Weeks, July 28, 1995.

67. Roberta Cohen, "Put Refugee Women in Charge of Food Distribution," in Bread for the World Institute, *Countries in Crisis* (Washington, D.C.: Bread for the World Institute, 1995), p. 35.

68. Kevin Ashley and Jason Matus, "Notes on Community-Based Relief Committees Used by WFP," June 1995, p. 1.

69. Ibid., p. 3.

70. Interview, Iain Levine, August 20, 1995.

71. Ashley and Matus, p. 5.

72. African Rights, "Imposing Empowerment," p. 29.

73. *SEOC Review*, 1995, p. 142.

74. Interview, Geoffry Loane, August 17, 1995.

75. *SEOC Review*, 1995, pp. iii–iv.

76. Interview, Geoffry Loane, August 17, 1995.

77. Interview, Andrew Natsios, September 25, 1995.,

78. Interview, Vincent Coultan, July 26, 1995.

79. Simon Simonse, "Human Rights and Cultural Values in Relief Operations in War-Torn South Sudan," mimeo, January 12, 1995, p. 5.

80. Adams and Bradbury, p. 47.

81. Macrae and Zwi, 1994, p. 315.

82. MSF, pp. 34–35.

83. Ibid., pp. 37–38.

84. Keen and Wilson, p. 217.

85. Iain Levine, "Discussion Paper on Political and Legal Implications of UNICEF's Role in Complex Emergencies," mimeo, 1995, p. 2.

86. Ibid.

87. Alex de Waal, "Emergency Work in the Nuba Mountains, Sudan," Abstract for European Working Group on the Horn conference, September 1995, p. 2.

88. Jim Bishop, InterAction Disaster Response Committee, memorandum, March 6, 1996.

89. Interview, Rowland Roome, August 7, 1995.

90. Interview, Geoffry Loane, August 17, 1995.

91. *SEOC Review*, 1995, p. 241.

92. Ibid., p. 156.

93. Natsios, "Humanitarian Relief Interventions in Somalia," p. 50.

94. Quoted in Levine, "Discussion Paper on Political and Legal Implications" p. 9.

95. African Rights, "Imposing Empowerment," p. 3.

96. Interview, Gordon Wagner, June 18, 1995.

97. This and the following two pages come primarily from Duffield and Prendergast, *Without Troops and Tanks*.

98. Interview, Matt Bryden, July 2, 1995.

99. Interview, Iain Levine, August 20, 1995.

100. Interview, Andrew Natsios, September 25, 1995.

101. Interview, Ted Chaiban, June 20, 1995.

102. Interview, Helge Rohn, August 17, 1995.

103. For more, see Prendergast, "The Gun Talks Louder Than the Voice."

104. Ken Menkhaus and John Prendergast, "The Political Economy of Post-Intervention Somalia," *CSIS Africa Notes* 172, May 1995.

105. Mark Bradbury, "The Somali Conflict: Prospects for Peace," Oxfam Research Paper No. 9, 1994, p. 4.

106. For more, see John Prendergast, "Sudanese Rebels at a Crossroads," Center of Concern Discussion Paper, 1994.

107. African Rights, "Imposing Empowerment," pp. 38, 47.

108. Catholic Relief Services, *Briefing Notes: Institutional Support for the Sudan Relief and Rehabilitation Association (SRRA)—The Third Wave* (Nairobi: Catholic Relief Services, 1995).

109. Wagner, "Project Proposal," p. 7.

110. John Prendergast, "Diplomacy, Aid and Governance in Sudan," Center of Concern Discussion Paper, 1995.

111. Interview, Constantinos Berhe, July 28, 1995.

112. I. W. Zartman, "Putting Things Back Together," in I. W. Zartman, ed., *Collapsed States: The Disintegration and Restoration of Legitimate Authority* (Boulder: Lynne Rienner, 1995), pp. 268–269.

113. Adams and Bradbury, pp. 47–48.

114. Interview, Rowland Roome, August 7, 1995.

115. Interview, Leenco Lata, June 29, 1995.

116. Interview, Gunter Schroder, July 28, 1995.

117. Mary Anderson, "Development and the Prevention of Humanitarian Emergencies," in Thomas G. Weiss and Larry Minear, *Humanitarianism Across Borders* (Boulder, Colo.: Lynne Rienner Publishers, 1993), p. 26.

118. Minear and Weiss, *Mercy Under Fire*, 195.

119. *SEOC Review,* 1995, pp. 244 and 254.

120. Ibid., pp. 92–93.

121. Ibid., pp. 93–94.

122. Ibid., pp. 95 and 225–226.

123. Interview, Ted Chaiban, June 20, 1995.

124. Interview, Iain Levine, August 20, 1995.

125. Levine, "Discussion Paper on Political and Legal Implications," p. 10.

126. Interview, Tim Leyland, July 5, 1995.

127. Stephen Jackson, "Trocaire Integrated Rehabilitation Program," draft mimeo for the Local Capacities for Peace Project, 1995, p. 21.

128. Interview, Rowland Roome, August 7, 1995.

129. Interview, Anisia Achieng, June 17, 1995.

130. Interview, Walid Musa and Matthew Bryden, July 10, 1995.

131. Interview, Geoffry Loane, August 17, 1995.

132. Minear and Weiss, *Mercy Under Fire*, p. 89.

133. Interview, Willet Weeks, July 28, 1995.

Chapter 5

1. Natsios, "Humanitarian Relief Interventions in Somalia," p. 57.

2. R. Jeffrey Smith, "U.S. Defies Allies, Grants $2 Million in

Humanitarian Aid to North Korea," *Washington Post*, February 3, 1996, p. A20.

3. Marc Michaelson, "Conflict Management Strategies for International Development Disputes," mimeo, 1994.

4. Adams and Bradbury, p. 32.

5. Marc Michaelson, "International NGOs: Prospects for Conflict Resolution Accompaniments to Relief and Development Assistance," mimeo, p. 1.

6. Kumar Rupesinghe, "Internal Conflicts in Africa: A Report on the London Seminar," *International Alert*, 1994, p. 3.

7. Adams and Bradbury, p. 10.

8. Ibid.

9. Hizkias Assefa, *Peace and Reconciliation as a Paradigm: A Philosophy of Peace and Its Implications on Conflict, Governance, and Economic Growth in Africa*, Nairobi Peace Initiative Monograph Series, No. 1 (1995), p. 4.

10. Excerpts from Larry Minear, *Humanitarianism Under Siege: A Critical Review of Operation Lifeline Sudan* (Trenton, N.J.: Red Sea Press, 1991), in *Life and Peace Review* 5, no. 1, p. 20.

11. Anderson, 1994, p. 22.

12. Macrae and Zwi, "War and Hunger," p. 31.

13. Iain Levine, "The Revitalization of Traditional Structures and Values in Southern Sudan: A Preliminary Proposal," mimeo, pp. 3–4.

14. Ibid., p. 4.

15. African Rights, "Components of a Lasting Peace in Sudan: First Thoughts," Discussion Paper No. 2, 1993, p. 25.

16. Ken Menkhaus, "Conflict, Peace-Building, and International Aid: The State of the Debate," *Life and Peace Review*, February 1995, p. 12.

17. Interview, Walid Musa, July 10, 1995.

18. Interviews with CRS staff, August 1995.

19. *SEOC Review*, 1995, p. 112.

20. Ibid., pp. 113–114.

21. Interview, Osman Ato, July 5, 1995.

22. Royal Anthropological Institute, p. 6.

23. Bread for the World Institute, p. 31.

24. Interview, Philip O'Brien, June 28, 1995.

25. Interview, Constantinas Berhe, July 20, 1995.

26. Keen and Wilson, p. 217.

27. Interview, Abdi Aden Ali, July 2, 1995.

28. Interview with UNDP staff, July 7, 1995.

29. Interview, Kabiru Kinyanjui, August 18, 1995.

30. Adams and Bradbury, p. 40.

31. Research on this process has been undertaken by Wal Duany and William Lowrey, funded by the U.S. Institute of Peace.

32. Menkhaus, "Conflict, Peace-Building, and International Aid," p. 11.

33. Interview, Heywood Hadfield, July 10, 1995.

34. Menkhaus, "Conflict, Peace-Building, and International Aid," p. 11.

35. Ibid., p. 12.

36. Ibid., p. 12.

37. Quoted in Smock, p. 15.

38. Adams and Bradbury, p. 37.

39. John Paul Lederach, *Building Peace: Sustainable Reconciliation in Divided Societies* (Tokyo: UN University, 1995), p. 121.

40. Adams and Bradbury, p. 35.

41. L. D. Brown, *Creating Social Capital: Nongovernmental Development Organizations and Intersectoral Problem Solving,* Institute for Development Research Reports vol. 11, no. 3, p. 1.

42. Ibid.

43. UNICEF, *Children and Women in Ethiopia,* 1993, p. 24.

44. Comments of Hugo Slim, in Royal Anthropological Institute, p. 21.

45. Interview, Iain Levine, August 20, 1995.

46. Keen and Wilson, p. 216.

47. Lederach, p. 121.

48. Interview, John Garang, June 26, 1995.

49. Interview, Askala Binega, August 10, 1995.

50. Interview with CRS staff, August 1995.

51. Ken Hackett, "Role of International NGOs and Civil Society in Preventing Conflict," speech to UN symposium on preventing conflict, April 1996.

52. Personal correspondence, Pierce Gerety, December 19, 1995.

53. Anne Hope and Sally Timmell, *Training for Transformation* (Harare: Mambo Press), 1987.

54. Sana'a (Yemen) Symposium on the Culture of Peace in Somalia (1995) *Draft Report,* paragraphs 14 and 16.

55. Andrew Natsios, *American Foreign Policy and the Four Horsemen of the Apocalypse* (Washington, D.C.: Center for Strategic and International Studies, 1996).

56. Eriksson, pp. 64 and 68.

57. *FEWS Bulletin,* January 26, 1996, p. 2.

58. Interview, Riek Machar, June 19, 1995.

59. Interview, Ahmed Mumin Warfa, July 1, 1995.

60. John Prendergast, "When the Troops Go Home: Somalia After the Intervention," *Review of African Political Economy,* vol. 22, no. 64, May 1995: 268–273.

61. InterAfrica Group, "Demobilization and Reintegration," Issues Note Number 2, December 1994, p. 8.

62. Ibid., p. 10.

63. Interview, John Garang, June 28, 1995.

64. Lederach, p. 70.

65. Interview, Eddie Johns, August 14, 1995.

66. Adams and Bradbury, pp. 60–61.

67. P. Collier and J. Gunning, "Policy Uncertainty, Repatriation and Investment," in P Collier, ed., *Some Economic Consequences of the Transition from Civil War to Peace* (London: Center for the Study of African Economies, 1994), p. 2.

68. P. Collier, "Demobilization and Insecurity: A Study in the Economics of the Transition from War to Peace," in Collier, ed., *Some Economic Consequences of the Transition from Civil War to Peace,* p. 2.

69. Ibid., p. 3.

70. Ibid., p. 10.

71. Quoted in Smock, p. 5.

72. Tardif-Douglin and Kumar, pp. 37–38.

73. UNICEF OLS (southern sector), "Review of 1994 Activities," p. 13.

Chapter 6

1. Interview, Philip O'Brien, June 28, 1995.

2. John Prendergast, "Tie Humanitarian Assistance to Substantive Reform," *The Washington Report on Middle East Affairs,* July/August 1995, p. 42.

3. Interview, Iain Levine, August 20, 1995.

4. MSF, pp. 7–8.

5. Ibid., pp. 8–9, 12–13.

6. Norman Barth, "'Tough Love' in the Horn of Africa?" *Life and Peace Review* 5, no. 1, 1994, pp. 25–26.

7. *SEOC Review,* 1995, p. 24 (citing Duffield and Prendergast, *Without Troops or Tanks*).

8. Interview, Tim Leyland, July 5, 1995.

9. Interview, Philip O'Brien, June 28, 1995.

10. Interview, Willet Weeks, July 28, 1995.

11. Interview, Geoffry Loane, August 17, 1995.

12. Interview, Kevin Ashley, June 24, 1995.

13. Interview, Rowland Roome, August 7, 1995.

14. Interview, Willet Weeks, July 28, 1995.

Concluding Thoughts

1. Eriksson, p. 69.

2. Hackett.

3. For the dangers of this phenomenon in the Angolan context, see John Prendergast and David Smock, "Angola's Elusive Peace," *CSIS Africa Notes* 182, March 1996.

Index

About the Book

Increasingly, questions are being raised about the effectiveness of humanitarian assistance and the extent to which it sustains or prolongs conflict. Whether aid actually lengthens conflict beyond its natural course is debatable; but it is indisputable that aid affects the course of conflict and has become integrated into conflict dynamics.

Prendergast explores these issues in the context of humanitarian assistance to Africa. He addresses three themes: how emergency aid can exacerbate conflict; how to minimize the negative consequences of aid; and how humanitarian aid might contribute to conflict prevention and peace building. He draws his evidence primarily from the Greater Horn—Ethiopia, Eritrea, Somalia, Djibouti, Sudan, Kenya, Tanzania, Uganda, Burundi, and Rwanda—a region that is now the focus of a major attempt by the U.S. government to reconceptualize bilateral and multilateral aid relations.

John Prendergast is visiting fellow at the University of Maryland's Center for International Development and Conflict Management and also Horn of Africa project director at the Center of Concern in Washington, D.C. His many publications include *Crisis Response: Humanitarian Band-Aids for Human Rights Crises; Civilian Devastation: Abuses by All Parties in the War in Southern Sudan* (with Jemera Rone); and *Without Troops and Tanks: Humanitarian Intervention in Ethiopia and Eritrea* (with Mark Duffield).